BRIGHT NOTES

BRAVE NEW WORLD AND OTHER WORKS BY ALDOUS HUXLEY

Intelligent Education

Nashville, Tennessee

BRIGHT NOTES: Brave New World and Other Works
www.BrightNotes.com

No part of this publication may be used or reproduced in any manner whatsoever without written permission, except in the case of brief quotations in critical articles and reviews. For permissions, contact Influence Publishers http://www.influencepublishers.com

ISBN: 978-1-645420-08-8 (Paperback)
ISBN: 978-1-645420-09-5 (eBook)

Published in accordance with the U.S. Copyright Office Orphan Works and Mass Digitization report of the register of copyrights, June 2015.

Originally published by Monarch Press.
Paul W. Gannon, 1965
2020 Edition published by Influence Publishers.

Interior design by Lapiz Digital Services. Cover Design by Thinkpen Designs.

Printed in the United States of America.

Library of Congress Cataloging-in-Publication Data forthcoming.
Names: Intelligent Education
Title: BRIGHT NOTES: Brave New World and Other Works
Subject: STU004000 STUDY AIDS / Book Notes

CONTENTS

1) Introduction to Aldous Huxley   1

2) Introduction to Brave New World   13

3) Textual Analysis

    Chapter One   19
    Chapter Two   23
    Chapter Three   25
    Chapter Four   30
    Chapter Five   33
    Chapter Six   35
    Chapter Seven   38
    Chapter Eight   41
    Chapter Nine   43
    Chapter Ten   44
    Chapter Eleven   46
    Chapter Twelve   48
    Chapter Thirteen   50
    Chapter Fourteen   51
    Chapter Fifteen   52
    Chapter Sixteen   54
    Chapter Seventeen   57
    Chapter Eighteen   58

4) Character Analyses   59

5) Critical Commentary   67

6) Essay Questions and Answers   71

7) Introduction to Point Counter Point   75

8) Textual Analysis

    Chapter One   78
    Chapter Two   80
    Chapter Three   81
    Chapter Four   82
    Chapter Five   83
    Chapters Six and Seven   85
    Chapters Eight and Nine   87
    Chapters Ten and Eleven   89
    Chapters Twelve and Thirteen   91
    Chapter Fourteen   93
    Chapter Fifteen   95
    Chapter Sixteen   96
    Chapter Seventeen   97
    Chapter Eighteen   98
    Chapters Nineteen and Twenty   99
    Chapter Twenty - One   101
    Chapter Twenty - Two   103
    Chapters Twenty - Three and Twenty - Four   104
    Chapters Twenty - Five and Twenty - Six   106
    Chapters Twenty - Seven and Twenty - Eight   108
    Chapter Twenty - Nine   110
    Chapters Thirty and Thirty - One   112
    Chapters Thirty - Two and Thirty - Three   113
    Chapter Thirty - Four   115
    Chapter Thirty - Five   117
    Chapters Thirty - Six and Thirty - Seven   118

9) Character Analyses	120
10) Essay Questions and Answers	124
11) Introduction to After Many A Summer Dies The Swan	126
12) Textual Analysis	
Part One	128
Part Two	140
Part Three	146
13) Character Analyses	148
14) Essay Questions and Answers	151
15) Introduction to Eyeless In Gaza	153
16) Textual Analysis	
Older, But Not Wiser (1933)	156
Trying to Find Himself (1934)	158
Childhood (1902 - 1903)	160
Approaching Middle Age (1926 - 1928)	162
The Young Gentleman (1912 - 1914)	163
17) Character Analyses	166
18) Critical Commentary	168
19) Essay Questions and Answers	172
20) Bibliography	174

INTRODUCTION TO ALDOUS HUXLEY

PREFACE

Aldous Huxley's writings express the disillusionment of the 1920s, the cynicism of the 1930s, and the questioning of the 1940s. Huxley was the product of the times, and his novels and essays are the expressions of his beliefs and concerns. Huxley's first two important novels, *Antic Hay* (1923) and *Point Counter Point* (1928), like T. S. Eliot's *The Waste Land*, express the despair and disillusionment of the period following World War I. By the time he wrote *Brave New World* (1932), he despaired of man's ability to save himself from himself. But thinking that he had found a possible solution to the dilemma of man, Huxley became interested in the teachings of Eastern mystics. His novel *After Many a Summer Dies the Swan* (1939) is a vehicle for many of his ideas; his collection of essays *The Perennial Philosophy* (1946) is a kind of anthology and commentary drawn from the writings of the mystics. Alexander Henderson (*Aldous Huxley*, London, 1935) was probably right when he said, "Huxley is primarily a light philosophical essayist using the novel form to present the more superficial modes of contemporary thought and feeling."

BIOGRAPHICAL SKETCH

Aldous Huxley was born on July 26, 1894, at Godalming, county of Surrey, England. His father was Leonard Huxley, a prominent literary man, and his grandfather was T. H. Huxley, a biologist who led the battle on behalf of the Darwinian evolutionary hypothesis. His mother was a niece of Matthew Arnold, the English poet, essayist, and critic. His family background seems to have prepared him for a variety of interests - everything from anthropology to zoology and from versification to mysticism. His brother Julian is a leading biologist, and Aldous at one time intended to follow a scientific career.

Having been educated at a preparatory school and at Eton, Huxley intended to become a doctor. But having contracted keratitis (an eye disease resulting in near blindness) he was forced to abandon this idea. He learned to read Braille; after two years he had recovered sufficiently so he could read with a magnifying glass. He then attended Balliol College, Oxford, studied English literature and philology, and took his degree in 1915.

It is interesting to note that Huxley considered the onset of eye trouble the most important single event in his life. This enforced isolation acted as a stimulant rather than a depressant - now more than he ever wanted to "see," know, and understand everything. And he did not want to "see" only what was apparent, but also what was implied. The following comment of Huxley seems to summarize this point of view, "My ambition and pleasure are to understand, not to act."

But it would be wrong to think that Huxley cut himself off from society in order to meditate and write. He and his wife (Maria Nys) traveled extensively and entertained frequently. They spent several years in Italy, had a cottage in France, visited

India and Central America, and finally settled in California. He was at home with many of the leading authors and critics of his day - Siegfried Sassoon, Wyndham Lewis, the Sitwells, and Robert Graves. He worked with John Middleton Murry on the staff of the *Athenaeum* magazine, and his friendship with D. H. Lawrence and his wife Frieda has been widely publicized. Some of the tremendous influence that his studies, his travels, and his friendships had on his work will be alluded to later.

Huxley published several volumes of poetry between 1916 and 1920, when he published *Limbo*, a collection of stories. In 1921 appeared his first novel, *Crome Yellow*, which established his reputation. At the same time he was writing articles, reviews, and essays for many periodicals. From the beginning of his literary career we can see his interest in fact and fiction - in poetry and prose. This compulsion to communicate - this desire to express his ideas and convictions on a variety of subjects and in a variety of ways - manifested itself until his death in 1963.

HUXLEY AS ESSAYIST

Huxley was a far greater essayist than he was novelist. Because he wanted to "say something," to make his ideas known, to influence others, his novels often suffer because they are too **didactic**. Whole sections of his novels could be published as essays since he often makes particular characters spokesmen for his ideas. It was only in the essay that he was free to say without embellishment what he thought and why he thought it. Many of the **themes** and ideas Huxley develops and expands in his novels were also expressed in his essays.

In his collection of essays *Do What You Will* (Doubleday, 1929), Huxley urges us to emulate the Greeks, to live a life which considers and accepts both the physical and spiritual elements of man, and to regard all manifestations of life as divine. At one point he says, "Man is multifarious, inconsistent, self-contradictory; the Greeks accepted the fact and lived multifariously, inconsistently, and contradictorily." In his novel *Point Counter Point*, the most admirable character and the spokesman for Huxley's ideas is Mark Rampion. In chapter nine, when speaking of the Greeks, he says, "They were civilized, they knew how to live harmoniously and completely, with their whole being.... We're all barbarians."

In another collection of essays, *Ends and Means* (Harper, 1937), he discusses the work of the Marquis de Sade, a French novelist and libertine: "de Sade's philosophy was meaningless carried to its logical conclusion. Life was without significance.... Sensations and animal pleasures alone possessed reality and were alone worth living for." In his novel *After Many a Summer Dies the Swan*, Huxley creates a character who lives by this philosophy and shows where this philosophy ultimately leads. The character, Jo Stoyte, wishes to find the secret of longevity so he will be able to continue his pursuit of the sensual life; when he discovers that the price of longevity is the loss of humanity, he indicates his willingness to revert to an animal state in order to retain the animal pleasures.

In another essay from the same collection Huxley discusses the change in values which resulted in the state achieving the highest value and significance to the detriment of the individual. "By the end of the twenties a reaction had begun to set in.... The universe as a whole still remained meaningless, but certain of its parts, such as the nation, the state, the class, the party, were endowed with significance and the highest value." His concern with this transfer of value from the individual to the state resulted in his brilliant **satire**, *Brave New World*. In Huxley's *Utopia* the individual exists for the state, not the state for the individual. A little further on he discusses the role science plays in our lives and questions the ultimate value of scientific advances. Since the **theme** of *Brave New World* is "the advancement of science as it affects human individuals," we can immediately see Huxley's concern with the use and misuse of science: "We are living now, not in the delicious intoxication induced by the early success of science, but in a rather grisly morning after, when it has become apparent that what triumphant science has done hitherto is to improve the means for achieving unimportant or actually deteriorated ends."

In another collection of essays, *The Perennial Philosophy* (Harper, 1945), Huxley is concerned with the meaning of existence - with the ultimate end of man. He says, "The last end of man, the ultimate reason for human existence, is unitive knowledge of the divine Ground [a spiritual Absolute - a God - without-form] - the knowledge that can come only to those who are prepared to `die to self' and so make room, as it were, for God." In his novel *Eyeless in Gaza*, Huxley recounts the spiritual pilgrimage of Anthony Beavis towards this end. As he meditates upon his life and his experience, Anthony suddenly understands the meaning and purpose of life, "And now at last it was clear, now by some kind of immediate experience he knew that the point was in the paradox, in the fact that unity was the beginning and unity was the end.... Unity with all being." Again Huxley states the same belief and the same idea in a novel and in an essay.

We might also look to the essays for specific comments which will help us to better understand Huxley as a novelist. Two quotations from "Vulgarity in Literature" (in *Music at Night*, Doubleday, Doran, 1931) are especially important. "Literature is also philosophy, is also science." A little further on he says, "I think it not only permissible, but necessary, that literature should take cognizance of physiology and should investigate the still obscure relations between the mind and its body."

HUXLEY AS A NOVELIST

The four novels discussed at length in this study guide illustrate many of Huxley's strengths and weaknesses as a novelist. The exuberance of his ideas, his use of wit and **satire**, the acuteness of his observations of mankind and its foibles, his juxtaposition of fact and fiction - these are his strengths. The shallowness of his characters, his overriding concern with teaching a lesson or pointing up a moral, the imposition at times of an overelaborate framework for the novel, the use of characters and situations which preclude "the illusion of reality" - these are his weaknesses. We can see certain of these strengths and weaknesses in each of the four novels.

Brave New World is Huxley's most popular novel, though not necessarily his most important novel. The reader is "swept along" by Huxley's vision of a Utopian future based on science and technology: he is dumbstruck by Huxley's clever juxtaposition of fact (scientific data) and fiction (future life on earth). The novel is logically developed - Huxley "begins at the beginning" with a detailed account of life in the new World State. But before long we realize that Huxley is not content simply to present a **satire** of present a future life and let the reader draw his own moral from the story. Instead Huxley allows his preaching to obtrude upon the fantasy he has created, and his characters soon become important only as spokesmen for particular ideas and beliefs.

In *Point Counter Point* Huxley has created a fantastic array of characters, but none is fully developed; each represents a particular point of view the author wishes to satirize. But there is much wit and humor in the novel and a variety of plots and counterplots which maintain reader interest. The elaborate musical analogy which is woven through the novel is at times distracting but does illustrate Huxley's considerable talent as a storyteller. And the two-angled view of life - the juxtaposition of the physical and the emotional, the esthetic and the scientific, etc. - contributes to the interest and the importance of the novel.

After Many a Summer Dies the Swan combines a highly sensational plot and outlandish characters in a wild and preposterous picture of the Hollywood scene. The caricatures of educators, starlets, doctors, and idealists provide some hilarious situations and some wry commentary on the temporary scene. But Huxley is not content to write a comedy - he creates Mr. Propter as a spokesman for his own ideas and beliefs. Unfortunately Propter is too good to be true, and his intrusions upon the scene tend to inhibit rather than enhance the value of the novel.

Eyeless in Gaza has been hailed not only as Huxley's most significant novel but also as one of the most important novels of the 1930s. In this novel Huxley uses flashbacks to recount one man's search for a meaning in life. The lack of a logical time sequence - the novel shifts backwards and forwards in time - is often distracting but is an attempt to show the unity of life and the unity and diversity of being. Huxley wished to show that an individual - his beliefs, ideas, and ideals - are the result of many influences. In this novel he recounts many of the influences that have molded Anthony Beavis. Perhaps this novel is most successful because it is in many ways a chronicle of Huxley's own search for a meaning in life.

Although Huxley wrote some ten novels, the four briefly discussed here are representative of the strengths and weaknesses of all of them. It is a pity that Huxley was not more concerned with the writing of fiction and less concerned with the expression of personal opinion. Huxley "rigged" his plots and "produced" his characters in order to convey some idea or express some concern - to him plot and characters were valuable only as "purveyors of truth."

THE NOVELS AS AUTOBIOGRAPHY

Because the novelist in some ways has to write about what he thinks, what he believes, and what he knows, every novel in some way may be considered autobiographical. Huxley is no exception. The people he knew, the places he visited, the books he read, the ideas he considered - all contributed to his development as a novelist, a skeptic, and a moralist, and often influenced what he wrote. Considering them in chronological order - *Point Counter Point* (1928), *Brave New World* (1932), *Eyeless in Gaza* (1936), *After Many a Summer Dies the Swan* (1939) - we can see some of the ways these novels reflect Huxley's own life and beliefs.

Huxley was disillusioned by the decadence of society and disgusted by the behavior of his class. *Point Counter Point* is a sardonic portrayal of the futility of life - each of the characters (with one exception) fails to be a harmonious adult. The one exception is Mark Rampion, who is an idealized version of D. H. Lawrence. (Huxley was much impressed by Lawrence and his beliefs, and they were close friends.) Huxley admitted that in some ways he was Philip Quarles and that the Notebook entries expressed many of his own ideas. Most critics consider that in the novel Denis Burlap is an unflattering caricature of Huxley's former editor, John Middleton Murry. Thus we see how circumstances, friends, and beliefs affected this work.

When he wrote *Brave New World* Huxley showed the extent to which his disillusionment with society and its values had influenced him. As noted in his preface to the New Harper edition, at the time the book was written he "toyed" with the idea that "human beings are given free will in order to choose between insanity on the one hand and lunacy on the other." And we might well consider that John the Savage's rejection of civilization in the World State paralleled D. H. Lawrence's rejection of the civilization he knew. Also, many of the ideas presented during the discussion in the last chapter of this novel echo many of Huxley's own views and concerns about the effect scientific advancement and technology would have on the individual.

Eyeless in Gaza is the picture of a man groping for a way of life that will bring meaning and purpose to his existence - in many ways it is a picture of Huxley and his change of attitude. In the novel Anthony Beavis changes from a self-indulgent, detached philosopher who sneers at life, to a humanistic pacifist who views life through the eyes of a lover. Huxley's own change of attitude was as remarkable - from a pessimist and portrayer of futility to a prophet and philosopher preaching mysticism. Both Anthony Beavis and Aldous Huxley find peace in Eastern mysticism.

After Many a Summer Dies the Swan is an exaggerated picture of the Hollywood Huxley knew when he lived and worked in California. In the person of Mr. Propter, Huxley has created a spokesman for his own ideas about the need for "liberation from personality, liberation from time and craving, liberation into union with God...." At the time he was writing this novel he was much affected by the views of Gerald Heard, a former science commentator for the British Broadcasting Corporation and an advocate of scientific humanism. Many of Mr. Propter's remarks seem to be taken directly from Heard's writings.

Huxley produced an amazing number of novels, essays, poems, short stories, articles, and reviews, as well as forewords, introductions, and prefaces for a variety of works ranging from a translation of the Hindu sacred book *Bhagavadgita, the Story of God* (Harper, 1951) to *Birth Control and Catholic Doctrine* (Beacon Press, 1959) and from *Studies in Hand-Reading* (Knopf, 1937) to *The Complete Etchings of Goya* (Crown Publishers, 1943). These titles indicate not only the wide range of Huxley's interests and abilities but also specific concerns he felt compelled to comment on. A study of all of Huxley's writings during a specific time period would indicate exactly what those particular interests, influences, and concerns were.

THE CONFLICT IN HUXLEY AND HIS WRITING

In *Texts and Pretexts* Aldous Huxley wrote, "The universe is vast, beautiful, and appalling." If any single sentence could be used to summarize Huxley's attitude, philosophy, and point of view, this might well be it. Huxley is aware of the conflicts within society, and within the individual, and he wants to make the reader aware of these conflicts. In his novels he often stresses the contrast and conflict by giving a two-angled vision of his characters and by considering an event in several aspects - emotional, religious, **metaphysical**, scientific. This multifaceted view of man, this concern with "unity in diversity," can be both a curse and a blessing for the reader.

A recurring **theme** in Huxley's novels is that of the young lover who is tortured by an irreconcilable conflict between romantic love and physical sexuality. We see this conflict in the love of the Savage for Lenina (*Brave New World*), Pete's feeling towards Virginia (*After Many a Summer*), Walter Bidlake and Marjorie Carling's relationship (*Point Counter Point*), and Brian Foxe's puritanical attitude regarding his fiancée (*Eyeless in*

Gaza). Since love is both spiritual and physical, involving both the mind and body, a dualism exists and persists.

Huxley has been subjected to much adverse criticism because of his fascination with the human body and its physical functions. His novels are filled with references to the bowels, the viscera, body odor, sickness, and disease at the same time that he is concerned with the mind and the spirit. Huxley wanted his reader to see that man is both body and spirit. He makes reference to the influence of the physical on the mental, the influence of the physiological condition of man on the psychological. As part of this "two-angled view" he often will consider both aspects of the same event. For instance, in *Point Counter Point* when Lord Edward hears the music of Bach, Huxley describes the process whereby the vibrations stimulate the auditory nerves, at the same time recounting the hearer's pleasure when he recognizes the melody.

Huxley discussed his "two-angled vision" in an interview with Ross Parmenter (*Saturday Review*, March 19, 1938). He said, "I try to get a stereoscopic vision, to show my characters from two angles simultaneously. Either I try to show them both as they feel themselves to be; or else I try to give two rather similar characters who throw light on each other...." Huxley was not especially successful in using this technique with two different characters because too often his characters can be labeled as "good guys" or "bad guys." Huxley's characters are too often "black" or "white" - only a few are "gray." Huxley is most successful when he uses the "two-angled" vision to show an individual in conflict with himself. Several good examples of the individual in conflict with himself occur in *Brave New World*.

The incongruous quality of life - its oneness and simultaneous diversity - is the basic emotional conception of

Huxley's philosophy. The following comment concerning Philip Quarles (Huxley's alter ego in *Point Counter Point*) might well summarize the dualism often alluded to in Huxley's novels: "... he felt convinced that the proudly conscious intellect ought to humble itself a little and admit the claims of the heart, aye and the bowels, the loins, the bones and skin and muscles, to a fair share of life."

BRAVE NEW WORLD

INTRODUCTION

Since its publication in 1932, *Brave New World* and its author have been the subject of much commentary and much criticism. Many people consider this Huxley's most important work: many others think it is his only work. This novel has been praised and condemned, vilified and glorified, a source of controversy, a subject for sermons, and required reading for many high school students and college undergraduates. This novel has had twenty-seven printings in the United States alone and will probably have twenty-seven more. A third generation is presently reading and discussing *Brave New World*. We might well ask, "What accounts for the continuing popularity of this novel?" Why does this work continue to attract attention and comment?" The answer lies in Huxley's skill as a writer - a writer of science fiction, a writer of social commentary, a writer with prophetic vision, a writer with a tremendous breadth and depth of interests and ideas, a writer of satire.

Brave New World is a masterpiece of science fiction. Huxley has imaginatively employed scientific facts and theories to produce a classic of its kind. This novel is in the tradition of Jules Verne, the French novelist who wrote *Twenty Thousand Leagues under the Sea* and *Journey to the Center of the Earth*, and H. G.

Wells, the English novelist who wrote War of the Worlds. Few writers of science fiction have equaled Huxley's ability to make the unbelievable seem believable and to make the improbable seem probable. His own interest in science, its use and misuse, its peril and its promise, contributed to the accuracy of his presentation and to the horror of his envisioned Utopia.

Huxley qualifies as a social commentator by reason of his diversified interests, his acquaintance with the great, the near-great, and the not-so-great. His comments are always perceptive, sometime biased, but never dull. He sees little chance of mankind saving itself; he sees mankind inexorably moving toward self-destruction. He sees himself as a voice crying in the wilderness - but crying to no avail, for the deaf refuse to hear.

The prophetic elements in *Brave New World* contribute much to its continuing popularity because year by year we see more and more of Huxley's fantasy becoming reality. Huxley himself later commented that we are moving in the direction of this Utopia much more rapidly than anyone could have imagined. At the time the novel was written only a comparatively few research scientists were concerned with conditioning, the importance of heredity and environment, and the effect of chemical imbalance on physical and mental development. Today, governments, educational institutions, and industries are exploiting the results of research in these areas.

The breadth and depth of Huxley's interests and ideas prompted one critic to refer to him as one of the most prodigiously learned writers of all time. In addition to his ten novels, Huxley wrote poetry, drama, essays, biography, and history. His interests and capabilities embrace art, religion, philosophy, music, history, politics, psychology - and this novel expresses Huxley's concern with the importance of each of these areas.

Huxley's **satire** expresses his profound pessimism. In *Brave New World* the only choice is between insanity on the one hand and lunacy on the other. In an early essay "Revolutions," he expresses this same pessimistic idea: "Now that not only work, but also leisure has been completely mechanized; now that, with every fresh elaboration of the social organization, the individual finds himself yet further degraded from manhood towards the mere embodiment of a social function; now that ready-made, creation-saving amusements are spreading an ever intenser boredom through ever wider spheres - existence has become pointless and intolerable. Quite how pointless and intolerable the great masses of materially - civilized humanity have not yet consciously realized." In *Brave New World* Huxley helps humanity to this realization.

AN HISTORICAL PERSPECTIVE

Some of the ideas and aspects of life in the World State of *Brave New World* are contained in several of Huxley's earlier works. In chapter five of *Crome Yellow*, which was published in 1922, Mr. Scogan speaks of a scientific Utopia: "... An impersonal generation will take the place of Nature's hideous system. In vast state incubators, rows upon rows of gravid bottles will supply the world with the population it requires. The family system will disappear...." By the time Huxley started to write *Brave New World*, the tremendous political, economic, and philosophical changes taking place in Europe and America contributed to his disillusionment.

On the international political scene we have the Bolshevik Revolution in Russia, the dictatorship of Mussolini in Italy, and the Nazi Party movement in Germany. Huxley had always been concerned about threats to man's freedom and independence. He realized that communism and fascism place the state above the individual and demand total allegiance to a cause. Recognizing the danger, he demonstrated the end result of this tendency in his fantasy.

At the same time there were tremendous economic changes in and between individual countries - more and bigger factories, more manufactured goods, the advent of mass-produced automobiles. Big business used and misused the individual - man became important as a producer and a consumer. Industry exploited the individual by molding him according to its image and likeness. Huxley goes one step further in his novel - man's chief importance is his ability to produce and consume manufactured goods.

With more and more people moving to the cities we see a change in attitude and point of view. As "one of the crowd" the individual is not responsible for himself or for anybody else - having lost his individuality he has also lost his respect for individuality. Huxley carries this loss of individuality one step further in his projection of scores of identical twins performing identical tasks.

Huxley was concerned when he saw these things happening because he saw them as very real threats to man's freedom and independence. His bitter satire results from his conviction that although man is able to do something about these threats to his freedom and individuality, he is unwilling to make the effort "to turn the tide." In the latter part of *Brave New World* Huxley discusses this shift in emphasis from truth and beauty to comfort and happiness.

SOME DEFINITIONS AND ALLUSIONS

A number of references, names, and **allusions** in *Brave New World* could be missed by the casual reader. Huxley draws upon his own extensive background in history, economics, and science and often assumes the reader is immediately aware of the significance of a particular word. Some of the more important of these words and concepts are discussed below.

Conditioning is defined as the training of an individual to respond to a stimulus in a particular way. The great Russian scientist Pavlov conducted experiments to determine how this conditioning takes place. Further experimentation has proven that individuals can be conditioned to respond in a predetermined way. In *Brave New World* individuals are conditioned to think, act, feel, believe, and respond the way the government wants them to.

Predestination is the act of deciding an individual's fate or destiny for him. Both the Old and New Testaments contain **allusions** to God as the Predestinator, but since the World State has eliminated God, predestination is now the function of a government bureau. In the World State each individual has been predestined according to the needs of society.

Thomas R. Malthus (the Malthusian belt) was an English political economist who propounded a doctrine on the theory of population. He believed that unless famine or was diminished the population, in time the means of life would be inadequate. In the World State mandatory birth-control measures are used to regulate the growth of population.

Ford was the most important figure in the formation of the World State. In a Christian society the life, work, and teachings of Christ are the source of inspiration and truth; in Huxley's Utopia the life, work, and teachings of Ford are the sources of inspiration and truth. Even time is reckoned according to Ford.

A.F. 632 is the year when these events take place. Since Huxley had projected his fantasy six hundred years into the future, by our reckoning the year would be approximately 2532 A.D.

Decanting is the name given to the completion of the artificial and mechanical stimulation of the embryo resulting in what we would call birth - an independent existence. Huxley details this process to emphasize the tremendous advancement of scientific knowledge and practice and to show the complete control of the individual from the time of conception.

THEME OF BRAVE NEW WORLD

In his foreword to the New Harper edition of *Brave New World*, Huxley states its **theme** as "the advancement of science as it affects human individuals." Within the last ten years we have seen tremendous advances in science and technology. In any single ten-year period since 1900 the advances in science and technology have overshadowed the advancement made during any previous hundred-year period. Huxley realized that these advances which were almost universally hailed as progress were fraught with danger. Man had built higher than he could climb; man had unleashed power he was unable to control.

Brave New World is Huxley's warning; it is his attempt to make man realize that since knowledge is power, he who controls and uses knowledge wields the power. Science and technology should be the servants of man - man should not be adapted and enslaved to them. *Brave New World* is a description of our lives as they could be in the none too distant future, if the present obsessions persist for standardization according to the sciences - eugenics and psychology, as well as economics and mechanics.

BRAVE NEW WORLD

TEXTUAL ANALYSIS

CHAPTER ONE

The novel opens with the Director of Hatcheries and Conditioning taking a group of students on a tour of the "Central London Hatching and Conditioning Centre."

Comment

We notice that the World State's motto is "Community, Identity, Stability." A World State would necessitate a single political ideology and a single point of view. This singleness of purpose emphasizes the need for conformity in social, political, and personal matters. The first part of the book discusses in detail how this stable society was established and is maintained.

Since babies in the *Brave New World* are "artificially" produced, the tour begins in the "Fertilizing Room." The students are shown the incubators where the male and female reproductive cells are kept. The year is A.F. 632.

> Comment

Huxley introduces us to several startling ideas at this point which he will develop in more detail as the story progresses. We learn that babies are artificially produced in a laboratory, and that the people have a new way of reckoning time.

The Director explains the process whereby a single human egg reproduces up to ninety-six identical twins. These individuals are mentally and physically identical and thus contribute to social stability.

> Comment

We begin now to understand better the motto of the World State: "Community, Identity, Stability." The World State controls every aspect of the person's life, including his conception.

Mr. Foster, one of the workers at the Centre, joins the tour. They enter the "Bottling Room" to continue observing the mechanical process being used to produce babies. The fertilized eggs are placed in bottles, labeled, and sent into the Social Predestination Room." The Director and Mr. Foster explain that a World Government bureau, the Predestinators, determines the number of each type of individual desired. Mr. Foster explains that the entire process from fertilization to maturity takes two hundred and sixty-seven days.

> Comment

Scientific knowledge is used extensively in this section. The Bottling Room process artificially reproduces much of the maturation process which normally takes place in the mother's womb. The two hundred and sixty-seven days is, of course, the normal gestation period.

Mr. Foster explains how the fetus (the child still in the womb) is predestined and conditioned according to the caste and adult life that has been selected for him. On the highest level are the Alphas, who will hold leadership positions, and at the lowest level are the Epsilons, who will do the simplest jobs in the World State. This conditioning begins at the time of fertilization and continues until decanting (birth). Conditioning prepares the yet unborn child for the kind of job he will do as an adult.

Comment

Society in the World State is determined by the government. The society consists of five main groups or castes: Alphas (leadership positions), Betas (positions demanding high intelligence), Gammas and Deltas (positions demanding some intelligence), and Epsilons (positions demanding no intelligence). Illustrations of the five types occur throughout the book.

The conditioning that takes place from the time of fertilization through the individual's formative years guarantees, in most cases, the individual's complete acceptance of every aspect of life in the World State. Since an individual, any individual, is conditioned by hereditary and environmental factors, if these factors are controlled, the individual may be controlled. And if an individual is conditioned to think, to act, and to react in a particular way to a particular stimulus, then free will has been abolished.

A government office in the World State determines the number and kind of individual needed in various positions and in various parts of the world. The Hatchery and Conditioning Centre is then given an order for a certain number of individuals with particular characteristics, abilities, and beliefs. In the words of the Director: "All conditioning aims at that: making people like their unescapable social destiny."

BRAVE NEW WORLD

TEXTUAL ANALYSIS

CHAPTER TWO

....

The Director and his students go to the "Infant Nurseries - Neo-Pavlovian Conditioning Rooms." Here the conditioning continues. At this time eight-month-old babies belonging to the Delta caste are being conditioned to hate books and flowers. The babies are frightened by loud noises and electrical shocks when they attempt to touch these objects; thereafter they will refuse to touch these objects.

Comment

The importance of conditioning is a scientific fact first proved by Pavlov, a Russian scientist; hence the reference to him in designating this area.

The Director explains that babies in the lower castes are conditioned to hate books and flowers because of the economic policy of the World State. In order to keep the factories busy and maintain a high level of employment, all classes are compelled to consume as many of the products of industry as possible - reading and nature study would not help the economy. One of the slogans based on their economic system is "The More Stitches, The Less Riches."

The Director tells the students that the principle of sleep-teaching dates from Ford's lifetime. This principle was later used to teach children the values they should hold. The group visits a dormitory where sleep-teaching is taking place, the two lessons for the day being Elementary Sex and Elementary Class Consciousness. These lessons teach the children to be happy in the group chosen for them. They learn that each group has its own color clothes and its own duties.

Comment

The conditioning that takes place influences the individual throughout his life. Since values can be taught, in *Brave New World* the values established by the World State are impressed upon the children. Many of these values are taught as slogans: "Ending is better than mending - A gramme (of soma) is better than a damn - Civilization is sterilization."

At the end of chapter two, one of the first uses of "Ford" instead of "Lord," or "God," or "Christ" occurs. Society in *Brave New World* is State-centered rather than God-centered. Since Ford has had, and continues to have, the greatest influence on their society, he is invoked as a supernatural being would be and is looked to as a source of inspiration and wisdom. We will see further reference to this substitution of Ford for God later in the book.

BRAVE NEW WORLD

TEXTUAL ANALYSIS

CHAPTER THREE

Going outside, the Director and his students watch six or seven hundred naked little boys and girls at play. Many of the children are playing simple sex games. The Director explains that at one time this sexual play had been regarded as abnormal and immoral.

Comment

This chapter contains considerable reference to sexual activity. We find that what the World State considers to be normal, we consider to be abnormal and immoral. Since Huxley makes many references to sexual activity, some explanation may be of value.

This *Brave New World*, through the advancement of science, has affected every aspect of the human individual's life. In some instances man's beliefs and values have been completely reversed or eliminated. Man is no longer responsible for himself - the state is his master. Man is simply "a cog in the wheel." Therefore, the individual uses sex as he would use a telephone, a spoon, a car - because it is needed at the particular moment. The individual must not "fall in love," marry, and raise children because this would demand allegiance to others, and the individual's allegiance is to the state only. The sexual license encouraged by the World State also eliminates emotional tension which may engender creative or destructive impulses. By removing tension and anxiety, the World State can better control its citizens.

The students find it difficult to believe that erotic play between children was once considered abnormal and immoral. A stranger arrives - it is the Resident Controller for Western Europe.

Comment

The rest of this chapter places characters in a variety of situations, and we are introduced to a number of new characters: (1) Mustapha Mond is the Resident Controller, one of ten World Controllers; (2) Bernard Marx is from the Psychology Bureau and does not seem to belong in the *Brave New World*; (3) Lenina Crowne, Fanny Crowne, Henry Foster, and the Assistant Predestinator work at the Centre.

Although Huxley has written this section to indicate that a number of things are occurring at the same time, it will be easier to discuss each conversation separately: the first conversation involving the Director, the Controller, and the students; the second involving Lenina Crowne and Fanny; the third involving the Assistant Director, Henry Foster, and Bernard Marx.

Notice Huxley's choice of names for his characters - Ford, Marx, Lenina, Benito Hoover. These have been chosen because of their **connotations** at the time the novel was written and their **connotations** today. Ford calls to mind Henry Ford, whose utilization of the mass-production technique has had a tremendous influence on social, political, and economic life. Marx is an obvious reference to Karl Marx, a German Socialist, whose greatest and best - known work, Das Kapital, expresses his belief that the fundamental factor in the development of society is the method of production and exchange. Lenina is a variation of Lenin - Nikolai Lenin, the Russian Socialist, who had a tremendous influence in the formation of the Union of Soviet Socialist Republics, the present-day Russia. Benito Hoover combines the names of two men who wielded tremendous power at the time Huxley was writing *Brave New World*-Benito Mussolini, the Italian dictator, and Herbert Hoover, the American President. Huxley's choice of names for his characters is significant because of his concern with the ways people are controlled - politically, economically, and socially.

The Controller recalls a saying of Ford that history is bunk. He speaks of "mother," "home," "family," "romance," and "love," and the students find such ideas and situations repugnant. He insists that stability is the most important thing for society and discusses the importance of conditioning. The Controller outlines the rise of Ford and the World State. Scientific progress has led to the abolition of old age, to innumerable distractions for everyone, to "no leisure from pleasure," to the elimination of thinking and worrying.

Comment

The importance of conditioning is shown throughout this section - the students find the idea of "normal family life" repulsive and the idea of motherhood embarrassing. They have been conditioned to consider their way of life superior, and they do.

The historical account of the rise of Ford and the World State provides the reader with some insight into how this society came about. Note Huxley's use of the inequalities of a democratic social system to show some reasons why this new society came about - poor housing, poverty, sickness.

Henry and the Assistant Director discuss the merits of Lenina Crowne as a sex partner. Bernard is upset by their conversation because of his own interest in Lenina. Henry and the Assistant Director advise Bernard to take Soma.

Comment

Although this is the shortest of the three conversations, it reveals much about Bernard Marx. Conditioning has not made him accept life as it is. He is not satisfied with his life and often refuses to take Soma, a drug which produces a feeling of happiness and well-being.

Lenina and Fanny discuss the men in their lives. Fanny is concerned because Lenina has been going out with only one man - Henry Foster. (Everyone expects a young woman to have sexual relations with many men because "everyone belongs to everyone else.") Lenina tells Fanny that Bernard Marx has invited her to visit the Savage Reservation with him, but Fanny is concerned because Bernard has the reputation of being odd (he does not conform).

Comment

The comments on the World State view of love are especially applicable to this conversation. Because the state considers any close relationship between two people could lessen the power and stability of the state, Fanny is concerned about Lenina's relationship with Henry. The state expects her to be "available" for anyone who wants her sexually; the state considers a person abnormal if he is not promiscuous.

While these conversations are taking place, the work of the Central London Hatchery and Conditioning Centre continues - the work of the World State goes forward.

Comment

Huxley's juxtaposition of past, present, and future in this chapter emphasizes the enormous control the World State exercises over the individual and every facet of his existence. The Controller discusses and explains the need for control and the methods of control; at the same time we see the results of this conditioning (control) in the thoughts, actions, and reactions of the other characters. And not content with simply explaining and illustrating, Huxley keeps referring to the continuing operations at the Hatchery and Conditioning Centre - producing tomorrow's citizens of the World State.

BRAVE NEW WORLD

TEXTUAL ANALYSIS

CHAPTER FOUR

PART ONE

On the way to the helicopter roof Lenina meets Bernard and tells him she wants to visit the Savage Reservation in New Mexico with him. He is embarrassed to discuss the trip with her in public. She leaves to meet Henry Foster and they fly to the Obstacle Golf Course.

Comment

This chapter makes reference to various castes in the World State: Henry and Bernard are Alphas; the lift (elevator) operator is an Epsilon - Minus; the Beta-Minus group is playing tennis; the Deltas are holding a gymnastic display and community sing; the Gamma girls are waiting for the tramcars. Each group has its own work and its own recreation.

PART TWO

Bernard, somewhat upset by his encounter with Lenina, rushes to his plane. He feels guilty and alone - he feels inadequate because he is shorter and thinner than others in the Alpha caste. Physically and emotionally he considers himself a misfit.

Comment

Huxley draws our attention to Bernard Marx because he does not look and act as a member of his caste should. He is short and slight when he should be tall and robust; he feels guilt and depression while others are happy; he is modest and unassuming rather than boastful and self-confident.

Bernard flies to Propaganda House to pick up Helmholtz Watson, a lecturer at the College of Emotional Engineering (Department of Writing). As on other occasions, Bernard and Helmholtz discuss their individualism and their desire to find some meaning in life.

Comment

Helmholtz is introduced at this point to indicate that the conditioning process is not always entirely successful. Although Bernard and Helmholtz are very different physically, psychologically, and emotionally, both are dissatisfied with life in the World State. What causes this dissatisfaction, they do not know, but somehow they sense that their existence is meaningless. Because they do not feel, act, and react in exactly the same way as others in their peer group do, both of them are being observed by their respective superiors.

Bernard is considered odd not only because he is physically smaller than the other members of the Alpha caste, but also because he likes to spend time by himself, and he does not like to participate in sport activities. (In the World State one should always be with others, always busy, never alone.) When discussing Bernard, reference is often made to the rumor that alcohol was accidentally put in his blood - surrogate - and this supposedly accounts for his oddness. Because individuals are decanted according to specification, any deviation would seem to be the result of some mistake, some chemical imbalance.

Helmholtz is suspect because he is too able, too intelligent, too successful. Because he is outstanding physically and mentally, because he is a good committeeman and a highly successful lover, he is an individual whose talent sets him apart - and the World State does not want extraordinary individuals; it wants "cogs in a wheel."

BRAVE NEW WORLD

TEXTUAL ANALYSIS

CHAPTER FIVE

PART ONE

On the way back from the golf course, Lenina and Henry fly by a crematorium. They discuss the social usefulness of all the castes and the fact that everybody is "happy." Landing on the roof of Henry's apartment house, they go down for dinner. Later, they spend the night in Henry's room, Lenina having taken the proper precautions to prevent pregnancy.

Comment

As at other points in the book, the necessity of doing things according to schedule and in a prescribed manner is stressed: the golf course and night club close at specified times; Lenina takes the contraceptive precautions specified by the regulations.

PART TWO

Every other Thursday Bernard has to attend a "Solidarity Service" at the Fordson Community Singery. He arrives a little late and takes a place in the group. Twelve men and women take alternate seats around the table. Soma tablets and liquid are taken as communion. As the Soma begins to take effect, individuals jump to their feet and shout as if in religious ecstasy. Although he feels nothing, Bernard acts his part. They all dance around the table shouting "orgy-porgy" in a kind of frenzy and then fall on the couches exhausted. Indiscriminate sexual relations conclude the "service."

Comment

The Solidarity Service takes the place of religious services and provides emotional release for the participants. But Bernard feels nothing - no rapture, no peace, no solidarity. He remains alone and unsatisfied.

Huxley's substitution of the Solidarity Service for the expected religious service re-emphasizes the extent to which the World State controls the people. The religious impulse in man has manifested itself through the ages; the World State recognizes this impulse and makes use of it. The Solidarity Service is a **parody** of and substitute for the Christian Communion Service; Soma is used to induce a "religious" feeling. Karl Marx called religion the opium of the people; in Huxley's *Brave New World* Soma is substituted for religion.

BRAVE NEW WORLD

TEXTUAL ANALYSIS

CHAPTER SIX

....

PART ONE

Lenina at first questions whether or not she should visit the Savage Reservation with Bernard Marx. She remembers his odd views - his dissatisfaction with his life, his desire to be different.

PART TWO

Bernard receives a permit to visit the Savage Reservation. The Director, who must sign the permit, tells Bernard of his visit there some twenty years before. He recalls that the girl who had accompanied him on the trip disappeared, and he had to return to London without her. While in the office, the Director reprimands Bernard for his odd behavior and warns him that conformity is necessary.

> Comment

The Director's account of his visit to the Savage Reservation becomes very important later in the book. In discussing Bernard's odd behavior, the Director uses an interesting term - "infantile decorum." People in the World State were expected to satisfy every desire without thinking - they were to be like infants, completely dependent on the state.

PART THREE

Bernard and Lenina arrive at the Reservation. The Warden attempts to impress them with statistics and tells them there is no escape from the Reservation for the sixty thousand Indians and half-breeds. Since the Savages have not been conditioned, they still preserve their old beliefs and customs (religion, marriage, natural birth, family life).

> Comment

Again we see the reversal in the values held by the World State. The Savages are considered uncivilized because they believe in marriage and morality as their ancestors had.

Bernard calls Helmholtz and finds that the Director of Hatcheries and Conditioning intends to replace Bernard and have him sent to Iceland because of his odd views and lack of conformity. Bernard and Lenina are given permission to enter the Reservation and are flown to the guesthouse.

Comment

In this chapter Huxley is preparing us for the contrast between life on the Reservation and life in the "civilized" part of the World State. Lenina recalls "truths" she has been taught - "A gramme in time saves nine" or "Progress is lovely" - and Bernard mockingly makes reference to the number of times this was repeated during conditioning to assure her acceptance of a particular idea. The Savages have not been conditioned; consequently they do not hold the same "truths." Their beliefs are based on tradition and what the Controller referred to as "old-fashioned" ideas about morality and right and wrong.

BRAVE NEW WORLD

TEXTUAL ANALYSIS

CHAPTER SEVEN

An Indian guide takes Bernard and Lenina to see the Savages dancing. Lenina is disgusted by the Savages - seeing evidence of old age, disease, and dirt horrifies her.

Comment

The things that horrified Lenina are the things that are not characteristic of the world she knows. The World State has abolished disease, marriage, motherhood, and old age everywhere except on the Reservations. (The government did not consider it worthwhile to "civilize" certain ethnic groups and certain remote areas of the World State.)

The drums, the singing, and the performance remind Lenina of the Solidarity Services. The dance continues, with the leader of the dancers throwing snakes to the others. The ceremony ends with the whipping of a young man. Lenina shudders at the sight of blood. Suddenly a young white man appears.

Comment

Lenina is distressed by the sufferings of the young man because she was conditioned to consider blood and violence disgusting, not because she feels sorry for him. The young man (John) tells Lenina and Bernard that his mother (Linda) came to the Reservation from the Other Place (London) with a man who was his father. The man was Tomakin, the Director of Hatcheries and Conditioning.

Comment

Bernard recalls the Director's story and realizes that knowledge of this affair with Linda could result in the Director's disgrace.

Lenina and Bernard meet Linda, who is a fat, ugly blonde. She is pleased to see them and recounts with horror that she, a Beta, had had a baby. She tearfully describes her life on the Reservation and speaks fondly of her life in the Other Place.

Comment

Huxley stresses the difficulty Linda had in adjusting to life on the Reservation since she had been conditioned to act and think only one way. She considers John "mad" because he accepts the Savage's values rather than hers.

Life on the Reservation contrasts violently with life in the Other Place. Here pain, suffering, disease, filth, and old age still exist - in the Other Place science has succeeded in abolishing anything which interferes with or impairs the physical well-being of the citizenry. We have already noted the contrast and conflict regarding morality.

Note that both ways of life are based on ignorance - an ignorance based on superstition or an ignorance fostered by the state. Huxley does not consider either way of life attractive or desirable because he believes that life should be conscious existence - a life based on reflection and study and an acceptance of one's own being.

BRAVE NEW WORLD

TEXTUAL ANALYSIS

CHAPTER EIGHT

Bernard finds the life that John, Linda, and the Savages lead unbelievable, and he asks John to explain it as far back as he can remember.

Comment

Although Bernard is considered odd because he does not conform blindly to life in the World State, he has known no other life.

John tells Bernard of the many men who visited Linda, the women who beat her because of her sexual activities, Linda's stories of life in the Other Place, his learning to read, and his life among the Savages.

Comment

The account of Linda's and John's life among the Savages underlines the differences between the two cultures. Linda, having been decanted and conditioned as a "Beta," had one set of values; the Savages, having maintained the "old ways," had a different set. John accepted the values, ideas, and ideals of the Savages.

Having received a superior education because of her caste, Linda was able to teach John how to read. And one of the books John acquired from Pope, one of Linda's male friends, was The Complete Works of William Shakespeare. His close reading of Shakespeare provided him with many ideas and beliefs and helped him develop a strong code of moral conduct.

Bernard tells John he will try to obtain permission for him and his mother to come to the Other Place (London). John is thrilled with the idea and, like Miranda in Shakespeare's The Tempest, exclaims, "O brave new world that has such people in it."

Comment

Huxley selects this quotation from The Tempest because of the parallel in the lives of Miranda and John: both are anxious to embrace a way of life that neither knows or understands.

BRAVE NEW WORLD

TEXTUAL ANALYSIS

CHAPTER NINE

After the horrifying events of their first day at the Reservation, Lenina takes a large dose of Soma and sleeps. Bernard contacts Mustapha Mond, the World Controller, and receives permission to bring Linda and John to London. John enters Lenina's room and finds her asleep, but he is too modest to touch her.

Comment

Bernard realizes that the return of John and Linda to London will assure his position and prevent his transfer to Iceland.

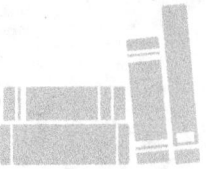

BRAVE NEW WORLD

TEXTUAL ANALYSIS

CHAPTER TEN

Bernard returns to London with Linda and John. The Director of Hatcheries and Conditioning, wishing to humiliate Bernard because of the unorthodoxy of his behavior, publicly announces his banishment to Iceland. Linda enters and exclaims that the Director is John's father; the crowd roars with laughter, forcing the Director to rush from the room.

Comment

Bernard realized that the presence of John and Linda in London would prevent any untoward action being taken because of his lack of conformity. The Director had hoped to use Bernard as an example of the consequences of nonconformity and had decided to make a public announcement. The arrival, of Linda and John (a physical manifestation of the Director's own unorthodoxy) saves Bernard.

This chapter opens with a rather detailed description of the work of the Hatching and Conditioning Centre - fertilization, predestination, decanting, conditioning. Then, in conversation with Mr. Foster concerning Bernard Marx, the Director says, "Unorthodoxy threatens more than the life of a mere individual; it strikes at Society itself." Thus our attention is again called to the necessity of conformity - the individual is not important, but the group is. Bernard's "crime" is his desire to do what he wanted to do instead of what they wanted him to do.

BRAVE NEW WORLD

TEXTUAL ANALYSIS

CHAPTER ELEVEN

....

Bernard becomes a celebrity and John a curiosity; Linda is content to take an extended Soma-holiday. Bernard takes the "Savage" to see many aspects of the *Brave New World*. At this point Lenina is attracted to John, but he ignores her.

Comment

A change takes place in Bernard in his new role as celebrity - he enjoys the attention he now receives. John is unimpressed by what he sees and still maintains his "old-fashioned" ideas and values; although attracted to Lenina, he considers such impulses immoral and represses them.

These tours which Bernard and John take provide descriptions of other aspects of life in the World State - specifically, the factory system and the educational system. Remembering that science has developed a method of producing up to ninety - six identical twins from a single egg, we see these identical automatons performing identical tasks. The upper-caste students (Alphas and Betas, each produced from a single egg) are not really educated - they are indoctrinated. In both situations individuality is nonexistent - each is but a member of a particular group.

BRAVE NEW WORLD

TEXTUAL ANALYSIS

CHAPTER TWELVE

....

Bernard invites many important personages to meet John, but John then refuses to attend. Having thus lost the friendship of these people, he turns again to John and Helmholtz.

Comment

Bernard realizes that his popularity is based on the curiosity others have about the Savage. He realizes that John and Helmholtz are his only "real" friends. At this point we find John reading Shakespeare to them - making them aware of new ideas, new beliefs, and new values which they find difficult if not impossible to accept.

This chapter emphasizes the difference in character of Bernard and Helmholtz, and their differences in point of view and attitude. Bernard's dissatisfaction with the life he is leading seems to stem from his not being accepted (alcohol in his blood -

surrogate), while Helmholtz's dissatisfaction seems to stem from his belief that life must have some meaning beyond the purely physical.

BRAVE NEW WORLD

TEXTUAL ANALYSIS

CHAPTER THIRTEEN

Lenina and John have "fallen in love," but she finds his desire to marry repulsive; she makes advances to him, and he locks himself in another room. The telephone rings, and John rushes from the apartment.

Comment

We see again the conflict between the two value systems - between the life on the Reservation and the life in the World State. Lenina and John are attracted to each other, but Lenina expects to have sexual relations with "no strings attached"; John considers sexual relations outside of marriage immoral and disgusting.

BRAVE NEW WORLD

TEXTUAL ANALYSIS

CHAPTER FOURTEEN

John arrives at the Park Lane Hospital for the Dying, where Linda has been sent. He sits by her bed, remembering his early life at her side, and weeps at her death.

Comment

The nurses at the hospital are mystified by John's reaction to Linda's dying; they cannot understand his being upset. Since close personal ties are forbidden and all were conditioned to accept death impersonally, they consider John's reaction indecent and disgraceful.

BRAVE NEW WORLD

TEXTUAL ANALYSIS

CHAPTER FIFTEEN

Saddened and enraged by Linda's death, John realizes that the government of the World State has made the people the way they are, and that they are being controlled; he warns those around him. Bernard and Helmholtz arrive, the police are called, and the three are taken away.

Comment

John recalls the words of Miranda in *The Tempest*, "O brave new world!" Having observed life in the World State, these words mocked him; now he hears them as a challenge to do something. He tries to warn those around him, but they refuse to listen - they do not want to change. Conditioning has made them unwilling or unable to desire freedom or to do anything to obtain it.

The difference in the reactions of Bernard and Helmholtz when they see the Savage pleading with the people to change emphasizes the differences noted earlier. Helmholtz sympathizes with John's comments on freedom and his desire to make others aware that the government of the World State has taken away their freedom, and he rushes to aid him. Bernard hesitates - he does not want to become involved.

BRAVE NEW WORLD

TEXTUAL ANALYSIS

CHAPTER SIXTEEN

....

Bernard, Helmholtz, and John are brought before Mustapha Mond, the World Controller. The Controller explains that since their society is organized for stability and happiness, individuality and free choice must be abolished. Both Bernard and Helmholtz are to be deported because of their unorthodox behavior and belief.

Comment

In this chapter Huxley makes known the Controller's ideas and, by inference, includes his own views of how the evolution of a World State is possible. The Controller's reference to the inability or unwillingness of the individual to act intelligently and reasonably, to the loss of individuality, and to the shift in emphasis from truth and beauty to comfort and happiness, gives emphasis to many of the comments made by thoughtful men about modern society. Huxley himself has commented on the possible consequences of these shortcomings of society in numerous essays.

Huxley believed that man was unable or unwilling to act intelligently and rationally. He was especially critical of the educated class because he believed they should take the initiative in bringing about needed social and political reform. The Cyprus experiment alluded to by the Controller seems to illustrate this point of view. In this experiment twenty-two thousand Alphas were given the opportunity to manage their own affairs - to use their superior intelligence to establish an ideal society. Within six years civil war broke out. Although given the opportunity to create a democratic Utopia, the Alphas were unable or unwilling to act independently, intelligently, and rationally, and chose, instead, to return to a system of rigid state control.

Note that in this chapter the World Controller addresses himself primarily to the Savage. Although dissatisfied with life in the World State, Bernard and Helmholtz do not know any other way of life nor any other values; only John and the Controller are able to discuss an alternate way of life and system of values. The Savage's questions about the value system of the World State and its inhabitants provide an opportunity for Huxley not only to summarize what has gone before but also to illustrate how the creation of an all-powerful World State is possible.

The Controller explains that even during the time of Ford (1932) there was a shift in emphasis from truth and beauty to comfort and happiness. The people were willing, even anxious, to bring about this shift. Mass production contributed to this shift since material goods were an important aid to comfort and happiness; when the masses seized political power, it was happiness rather than truth and beauty that mattered. Once the choice had been made, truth and beauty, art and science, were seen as threats to universal happiness since such inquiry can lead to dissatisfaction with the status quo. Most people are happy when they get what they want and never want what they can't get. In the World State of A.F. 632, the government provides what the people want and through conditioning prevents them from wanting what they can't have. Anyone who becomes "too self-consciously individual to fit into community life" is sent to an island lest he "contaminate" the others.

BRAVE NEW WORLD

TEXTUAL ANALYSIS

CHAPTER SEVENTEEN

The World Controller and the Savage are left alone and discuss God and philosophy. The Controller again declares that a stable society is possible only if all conflict, internal and external, is abolished - God and modern society are incompatible.

Comment

Huxley, through the World Controller, says that modern man has chosen machinery and scientific medicine and universal happiness instead of God, has chosen them as substitutes for God and the religious impulse. This reference to God and the religious impulse embraces all the attributes and aspects of a human being that make him noble and fine and heroic; in the words of the Savage, "I want God, I want poetry, I want real danger, I want freedom, I want goodness, I want sin." Huxley believed that since man was composed of body and soul, flesh and spirit, his life should reflect this dichotomy. Modern man's values often glorify the body and deny the spirit.

BRAVE NEW WORLD

TEXTUAL ANALYSIS

CHAPTER EIGHTEEN

Bernard and Helmholtz are leaving London, but the Controller has forced the Savage to remain in the area. Seeking refuge in an abandoned lighthouse, the Savage attempts to resume his old life. He disciplines himself severely to remove the taint of the *Brave New World*, but the curious come to watch his strange antics and disturb the solitude he seeks and needs. Finally, in despair, he hangs himself.

Comment

The Savage attempted to duplicate his old life and his old ways - working with his hands and disciplining his mind and his body. But he could not remove the horror and corruption within or without - he could not forget Lenina, and he could not find peace and solitude. When he could no longer control his thoughts, when he could no longer be an individual, he killed himself. In the World State the choice is conformity or annihilation.

BRAVE NEW WORLD

CHARACTER ANALYSES

Director Of Hatcheries And Conditioning

The Director of the Central London Hatchery and Conditioning Centre is the first character we meet; the novel opens with the Director taking a group of students on a tour of the Centre. Note that the Director (Tomakin) is, with but two exceptions, always referred to as the Director. This emphasis on the "function" of the man is appropriate since his primary concern is the production of automatons to populate the *Brave New World.*

The Director is an Alpha-plus, and because of the importance of his position we might well assume that he is a very intelligent and capable man. His comments during the tour indicate that he is efficient, very businesslike, somewhat officious, and very much concerned with conformity - "The primal and the ultimate need. Stability." In fact, when the World Controller mentions history (a forbidden subject), the Director is somewhat taken aback; he recalls with some dismay the rumors that old forbidden books were hidden in a safe in the Controller's study.

Perhaps one reason Huxley portrays the Director as very conventional and scrupulously correct is to stress the **irony** of the Director's unconventional behavior apparent in his previous relationship with Linda. Imagine the horror and confusion he felt when everyone realizes that he is a father (horrible word). Because the Director had disgraced himself by the impropriety of his actions, he resigns. Bernard becomes a kind of hero, and we hear nothing of the Director again.

Henry Foster

One of the standard men and women who work at the Hatchery, Henry is proud of his work. He is efficient, intelligent, and, most important, "conventional." Henry does everything he is expected to do and does it well - in every way he is an ideal citizen of the World State. In the bureaucracy of the World State he is the young man "with a future" - he knows what is expected of him and does it. Henry Foster would not be classified as an important character in the novel since he does not initiate or determine action - he is most often seen as Lenina's sometime lover.

Mustapha Mond, A World Controller

As one of the ten World Controllers, Mustapha Mond provides considerable information about the creation and maintenance of the World State. He is an intelligent, capable, good-natured man whose dedication and ability we must admire even if we do not approve. His comments at the beginning of the novel, when he meets the Director and the students provide not only information about his role in the World State but also reveal something of his character.

The World Controller is one of the most important characters because he is the most intelligent and the most knowledgeable - he has read and studied the Bible, Shakespeare, history, philosophy (all forbidden books). As a young Alpha-plus, his own unconventionality necessitated a choice between life on an island (reserved for those who were "too self-consciously individual to fit into community-life") and life in the World State (being "taken on the Controller's Council with the prospect of succeeding in due course to an actual Controllership.") Because the Controller has freedom of choice - a freedom which conditioning normally inhibits or destroys - he is one of the few real individuals we meet in this novel.

In the latter part of the novel the conversation between the Controller and John the Savage is the device Huxley uses to "put across" his own ideas and concerns. When the Controller explains his values and beliefs, his arguments and explanations are clearly and logically presented; his sanity makes the insanity of the *Brave New World* all the more vivid and frightening. The Controller in many ways represents the intelligent, capable individual who uses his intelligence and capability for unworthy ends.

Bernard Marx

Because he is different, Bernard is the source of considerable speculation and suspicion. He does not enjoy sports (everyone is expected to); he likes to be alone (others like crowds); he is unhappy (everybody else is happy). Bernard doesn't know why he is dissatisfied, why he is different; many of his associates speculate that alcohol was accidentally put in his blood-surrogate while he was still "in the bottle."

When we first meet Bernard we see him as a rebel, a protestor, "an individual." He wants to stand up for his rights, to battle against the order of things. We later learn that Bernard questions the conformity of life in the World State and the values it teaches, but that his dissatisfaction seems to stem from his not being accepted. When he returns from the Reservation with John and Linda, he becomes a kind of hero, the girls who formerly ignored him become attentive, important personages in the World State curry his favor, and Bernard is happy and enthusiastic about his life in the World State.

Huxley indicates that Bernard's protest is not intellectual or moral, but personal and social; he willingly accepts life in the World State when he is accepted. When the novel ends we find that Bernard's fortunes have changed and he is to be deported to Iceland because of his nonconformity. Bernard protests his innocence, begs the World Controller to reconsider, and finally is carried out still shouting and sobbing.

Lenina Crowne

Young and pretty, Lenina is very popular as a sex partner, but she sometimes finds living the motto "Everybody belongs to everybody else" a little tiring. She is a happy, contented, well-adjusted citizen of the World State; she accepts its teachings and values without question. The only disconcerting element in her life is the frustration brought about by her feelings for John the Savage. Lenina finds John attractive and attempts without success to seduce him. She cannot understand his attitude regarding sex even as he cannot understand hers. Fortunately she, like the others, can escape most frustrations and unhappiness by taking Soma.

Lenina is a fairly important character because she is instrumental in bringing about the suicide of John the Savage, although we cannot in any way blame her. (She is a product of the system, and the system is wrong.) Because she is a beautiful, desirable woman, she personifies for John the conflict between the body and the spirit. In a way she repeats the conflict he felt regarding his mother - he is at one and the same time attracted and repelled by the object of his affections.

Helmholtz Watson

Intellectually, socially, and physically the ideal of his Alpha-plus caste, Helmholtz is regarded with some suspicion by his associates because he is too perfect. Like Bernard he questions the conformity of life in the World State and the values it teaches, but, unlike Bernard, his dissatisfaction stems from his feeling that there must be more to life than mere physical existence. Although not as important to the development of the novel as Bernard, Helmholtz is in many ways a more admirable character because, instead of simply talking about what he believed, he acted.

As noted earlier, in this novel Huxley expressed his pessimism regarding man and his ability to save himself; consequently none of the characters is able to bring about change. However, Helmholtz is at least willing to try. When the Savage tries to tell the people they are being controlled, Helmholtz joins forces with the Savage when a melee breaks out. Later he accepts his banishment with considerable aplomb and asks that he be sent to a cold climate since he feels such discomfort might aid his writing.

Linda

Having been decanted and conditioned a Beta and then forced by circumstances to spend some twenty years on the Reservation, Linda offers some interesting comments and contrasts. At the Reservation she is not accepted because her values and beliefs are those of the Other Place - when she returns to London, people find her repulsive and ignore her because she is fat, old-looking and unattractive. Having been conditioned a Beta, Linda cannot understand or adapt herself to life on the Reservation. But since the Reservation does not have the ultramodern medical facilities which help retard physical decay, she has grown old even as the Savages do. Her relationship with John is also ambivalent - she is horrified at the idea of being a "mother" and yet she admits that John has been a great comfort to her. Her death during a Somainduced stupor finally provides release.

John The Savage

A curious mixture of the "old" world and the "new," John does not belong to either. He is not accepted by the Savages on the Reservation because he is "different," and he cannot and will not accept the life and values of the Other Place (London). Like Bernard, Helmholtz, and Linda, he doesn't belong - he is an alien, a misfit, a "mistake."

John is the most important character in the book because he acts as a bridge between the two cultures, and having known both "ways of life" he is able to compare them and comment on them. His beliefs and values are a curious mixture of Christian and heathen, of "Jesus and Pookong," but, most important, he has a strict moral code. His "old fashioned" beliefs about God and right and wrong (his beliefs closely duplicate Christian morality) contrast sharply with the values and beliefs of the citizens of the *Brave New World* ("God isn't compatible with machinery and scientific medicine and universal happiness"). It is this conflict between the two value systems that ultimately brings about his suicide.

When we are first introduced to John and the Reservation Huxley makes us aware of the moral conflict, but he also makes us aware of the social and emotional conflicts. The social conflict results from his not belonging on the Reservation; his mother was the white she-dog despised by the Savages. The emotional conflict results from the attraction and repulsion he feels towards his mother - he loves her but finds her promiscuity revolting. And, too her stories of the Other Place (London) fill him with wonder and a vague discontent.

The arrival at the Reservation of Bernard and Lenina and the Savage's subsequent arrival in London contribute to the conflict he already feels. John is attracted to Lenina but feels that such lustful feelings are wrong and must be repressed; Lenina is attracted to John and cannot understand the Savage's reticence and unwillingness to show any interest in her. Finally when John protests his love and expresses his desire to marry her, Lenina considers such an entanglement absurd and scoffs at the idea. But John is unable to put her out of his mind. His love for her finally breeds hatred, and when this hate turns inward upon himself, the Savage hangs himself.

Like the others in this novel, the character of the Savage is not believable. (Huxley was not interested in creating characters; he was interested in expressing ideas.) The Savage speaks too intelligently and reasons too well for one whose education consisted of reading a few books and talking to practitioners of a combination fertility - Penitente cult. Huxley himself admitted the inconsistency. But if we accept John simply as a spokesman in another of Huxley's novels of ideas, he is more than satisfactory.

Because *Brave New World* is both fantasy and **satire**, Huxley's characters are both fantastic and satirical. They are exaggerated because the year is A.F. 632; they offer a caustic commentary because more often than not they express what we must recognize are twentieth century viewpoints. At this time (1931) Huxley was completely disillusioned with mankind and with its choice of values or lack of values - he saw no hope for man's ultimate salvation of himself. He expresses his pessimism by offering no glimmer of hope in his novel. None of his characters is able to change or to bring about change.

BRAVE NEW WORLD

CRITICAL COMMENTARY

COMMENT ON BRAVE NEW WORLD

Although Huxley published ten novels, four of them after the appearance of *Brave New World*, not one of them attained the popularity or provoked the commentary occasioned by this novel. Huxley's title continues to be a catchword-writers and speakers often employ it to express concern or disdain for the direction society has taken, or for its lack of direction. But many readers and critics still consider, as they have for some years, that this novel is simply an above-average example of science fiction or an entertaining fantasy. Too few were willing or able to see that Huxley meant *Brave New World* to be a warning - a warning that a World State is not only possible but probable if we do not protect the rights of the individual to be an individual: to be unique and free.

In the *New York Times* (February 7, 1932) review of this novel, the reviewer said, "It is Mr. Huxley's habit to be deadly in earnest. One feels that he is pointing a high moral lesson in satirizing Utopia. Yet it is a little difficult to take alarm ..." This comment might well be considered typical - it is difficult to take alarm when we think, believe, and feel that Progress Is Our Most Important Product. However, Huxley believed that the Individual, not Progress, was most important. For this reason he tried again and again in numerous ways to warn that progress should not and must not be made at the expense of the individual.

As noted in the Introduction, Huxley wrote essays, poetry, short stories, and biography in addition to his novels. Following the publication of *Brave New World*, Huxley continued to expand his ideas and to caution his readers in numerous essays and in his novel *Ape and Essence*. This novel explores still other possibilities of the future, but it was not nearly as successful as a novel nor as an instrument of propaganda. It is in a collection of essays on freedom, *Brave New World Revisited*, that Huxley most succinctly and lucidly presents his concerns and beliefs.

BRAVE NEW WORLD REVISITED

Lest we should dismiss *Brave New World* as a fantasy, a Utopian novel, or a pessimistic view of the modern world, Huxley entitles his collection of essays on freedom, *Brave New World Revisited*. Huxley was concerned that readers, critics, and commentators could not or would not accept his novel not only as a **satire** on the life and values of the time (1931) but also as a warning of what the future could hold for mankind. Consequently these comments on the contemporary scene (1958) were dubbed a "revisit" to emphasize that in some ways, in too many ways, the *Brave New World* is already upon us.

In his introduction to these essays Huxley says, "The subject of freedom and its enemies is enormous, and what I have written is certainly too short to do it full justice, but at least I have touched on many aspects of the problem." In his novel he employs **satire** to warn mankind; in his essays he employs reason - having used fiction, he turns now to facts and opinions. Huxley includes comments on overpopulation, overorganization, propaganda, and persuasion, and discusses what can and should be done since "without freedom, human beings cannot become fully human."

In *Brave New World* Huxley opens his novel with a discussion of biology; he begins at the beginning. Consequently, or at least subsequently, his collection of essays begins with a discussion of overpopulation and its consequences. In the World State population was controlled as an aid to social stability; in his first essay Huxley warns that overpopulation can lead to economic insecurity and social unrest which, in turn, foster greater government control. The population explosion poses many problems for mankind - of late, economists, politicians, and social scientists have issued warnings and dire predictions. If this growth remains unchecked, individual freedom may be impossible, for as the population increases, so does the need for organization. The greater the population, the greater the work force, and so also the greater the concentration of political and economic power. Today in the United States one out of ten people work for the government in some capacity, and a comparatively few industries control the country's economy. Huxley warns us that the concentration of power in the hands of the few may lead eventually to the regimentation and exploitation of the many. "Too much organization transforms men and women into automata, suffocates the creative spirit and abolishes the very possibility of freedom." This emphasis on the importance of the group rather than the individual is discussed at length in William Whyte's *The Organization Man*.

Today newspapers, magazines, radio, and television make possible a wide dissemination of propaganda in an effort to persuade people to support or adopt a particular opinion, attitude, or course of action. This propaganda may be consonant with enlightened self-interest or an appeal to passion; in every case it is an attempt to mold or move the individual in some way. Those who control mass media, who control propaganda, exercise tremendous control over the individual. Today the advertiser and the politician use the mass media to influence opinion, attitude, or course of action; in the future the mass media might be used to control opinion, attitude, or course of action as in *Brave New World*.

In his discussion of the various forms of persuasion, Huxley includes chemical persuasion, subconscious persuasion, and sleep-teaching. The World State provided Soma to insure happiness; today tranquilizers offer release form tension and emotional stress. Today "subliminal projection" is a subtle from of conditioning since people are subconsciously influenced to act in a predetermined manner. Since an individual is susceptible to suggestion, sleep-teaching was used in the World State to condition an individual according to government specifications. Huxley warns that all three forms of persuasion are effective and have the potential for good or evil.

Huxley does not end his essays on a pessimistic note - at that time he believed we could save ourselves if we wanted to. That is the key. If we are complacent, indifferent, uninterested in our future - he believes the future is not worthwhile. But if we are willing to search for answers and to work out solutions - then the individual and individuality can be saved.

BRAVE NEW WORLD

ESSAY QUESTIONS AND ANSWERS

Question: What is the **theme** of *Brave New World*?

Answer: In Huxley's own words, the **theme** of *Brave New World* is "the advancement of science as it affects human individuals." In 1931, when he was writing his novel, each advance in science and technology was being hailed not only as evidence of man's progress but also as the hope of man's future. Huxley felt that this unqualified praise of science was wrong, that man's advances in science and technology were fraught with danger, that the misuse of knowledge results in evil, not good. Projecting his novel into the future he offers a picture of the world as it might become if Man becomes subservient to Science rather than Science subservient to Man.

Question: What is the significance of Huxley's title?

Answer: Huxley's title is taken from William Shakespeare's *The Tempest* (Act V, Scene 1) and occurs in a speech of Miranda: "How beauteous mankind is! O brave new world that has such people in it." Having been exiled on an island with her father, the deposed Duke of Milan, Miranda makes this remark when she sees other human beings for the first time. Ironically these same people had plotted against her and her father, had planned for their ultimate destruction, and had attempted murder but a short while before she sees them for the first time. But she is so overcome by the wonderment of what she is seeing for the first time that she calls "good" that which is potentially or actually evil. Huxley likens those who consider scientific advancement an unsullied good to Miranda - both are mistaken in their assumptions but blissfully happy in their ignorance.

Question: What is the significance of Huxley's use of "Ford" as a substitute for "Christ" or "God"?

Answer: In the *Brave New World* science and technology have replaced God as a source of value and meaning in life. Because Huxley believed that this shift in emphasis was given great impetus when Henry Ford revolutionized manufacturing with his assembly line technique, the introduction of the Model-T Ford is used as the opening date of the new era. This change in emphasis is symbolized by the changing of the Christian Cross to the Ford T. In the words of the World Controller, "God isn't compatible with machinery and scientific medicine and universal happiness."

Question: In his novels Huxley often uses a spokesman for himself and his ideas. Who is his spokesman in this novel?

Answer: John the Savage and Mustapha Mond, the World Controller, present many of Huxley's ideas and beliefs. Their discussion in chapters 16 and 17 acts as a summary of the book. Mustapha Mond by reason of his position had access to "forbidden books" and was therefore aware of the "old beliefs and ideals." John was acquainted with the works of Shakespeare and the religious practices of the Savages and could therefore question the values of the World State. By these questions and answers, explanations and discussions, Huxley is able to express his fears about, and to offer his commentary on, the contemporary scene.

Question: Why was society in the World State divided into castes?

Answer: Every society needs individuals with different talents and capabilities to perform different functions - teachers and garbage collectors, bankers and elevator operators, lawyers and gardeners, scientists and factory workers. Since a stable society was the aim of the World State, the caste system provided a stabilizing influence. An individual was predestined to serve in a specific capacity according to the particular needs of the time. Since the individual had been decanted and "conditioned" physically and psychologically to perform a specific task, he functioned happily in that capacity. For instance, a Beta was happy because he didn't have to work as hard as an Alpha and because he was smarter than the others; an Epsilon was too ignorant to be unhappy.

Question: What is the significance of the World State's motto: "Community, Identity, Stability"?

Answer: The World State's motto emphasizes the importance of the group and the subsequent unimportance of the individual. Community stresses the importance attached to the individual as a contributor to society - "Everyone belongs to everybody else." Reference is made to the contribution the individual makes even after death - the body is cremated and the phosphorus thus obtained is used as fertilizer. Identity refers to the various classes (castes), their specialized duties, and their distinguishing uniform. A particular character is often spoken of as a Beta or an Alpha as a means of identification. In the lower classes identity was stressed even more since there might well be ninety-six identical twins performing a particular task in a single factory. Stability is the key word in the World State. Decanting and conditioning, the abolition of the family, and conformity in thought and action - all contribute to a stable society.

Question: Why does Huxley have John the Savage commit suicide?

Answer: Huxley had John commit suicide in order to show the hopelessness of life in the *Brave New World*. Not only was John unable to accept a life founded on conformity and the pleasure principle ("no leisure from pleasure") but there was also a conflict within himself because of his ambivalent feelings towards Lenina - he found her desirable but considered such feelings sinful. Because the World Controller would not allow John to return to the Reservation, he tried to duplicate his "old" life, to be self-sufficient, to avoid being contaminated by life in this Other Place, to forget Lenina. But his hiding place was discovered; he became a curiosity; people came and laughed at his curious ways. One day Lenina came by with Henry; the Savage cursed her and himself. He struck out at her with a whip and then beat himself in an attempt to dispel his lustful feelings. The crowd took up a chant - "Orgy-Porgy." The Savage joined the others in the orgy. In the morning he realized what had happened and committed suicide.

POINT COUNTER POINT

INTRODUCTION

In his title, *Point Counter Point*, Huxley indicates his intention to use the vocabulary and characteristics of music to develop his novel. Although not entirely successful because of a number of discordant elements, the novel is an attempt to use an elaborate musical framework as the vehicle for his ideas. The musical term for a title, the interweaving of characters and themes, and the division of the novel into symphonic movements are attempts to integrate totally the analogy between music and life.

The term point counter point refers to the matching of one "point," as notes were previously called, with the corresponding point, or note; it is the art of combining several melodies, or parts, simultaneously. Huxley in his novel matches the decisive points in the lives of his characters in this manner. In chapter three, he has Lord Edward remark how the life of the universe is like music with harmonies and counterpoint and modulations.

At Lady Edward's musical party we are introduced to the main characters. A musical background is provided - the blending of the characters duplicating the blending of the instruments. Each of Huxley's characters embodies a single idea, a dominant characteristic, a special use, and each is utilized in a particular way to achieve a particular effect. Likewise, certain themes predominate - a number of characters, a number of instruments, are introduced to form a particular pattern and add to the desired effect.

To carry out the musical analogy, the novel can be divided into the four movements of a symphony. The opening **theme**, which predominates throughout, is played by Marjorie Carling and Walter Bidlake. This first movement - slow and sedate (andante) - provides needed background information. At about chapter thirteen a faster tempo (allegro) marks the beginning of the second movement; we move swiftly from one situation to another. Sidney Quarles' appearance in chapter twenty marks the beginning of the third movement - Huxley creates situations for his characters which are both satirical and playful (scherzo). The fourth movement (rondo) concludes with a brief reference to previous movements; a fitting **climax** to the work as a whole is provided by Burlap and Beatrice in the bathtub.

If this recounting of Huxley's use of analogy seems somewhat forced and farfetched, it is altogether fitting and proper that it should be so. As a piece of literature the novel suffers at times when Huxley belabors the analogy. (Only the musical analogy is coordinated and completed.) The novel's uncoordinated structure helps convey its **theme** - society divided into individuals without common beliefs and each following his own desires without regard for others. The discontinuity of the novel matches the discontinuity of life.

A letter written by D. H. Lawrence to Aldous Huxley emphasizes the importance of this novel: "I do think you've shown the truth, perhaps the last truth, about you and your generation, with really fine courage. It seems to me it would take ten times the courage to write *P. Counter P.* that it took to write *Lady C.* and if the public knew what it was reading, it would throw a hundred stones at you, to one at me." Remembering the furor and indignation *Lady Chatterly's Lover* continues to cause, we can appreciate Lawrence's remarks. *Point Counter Point* is a scathing indictment of a whole generation and of a whole way of life.

In chapter three Huxley quotes from the writings of Claude Bernard, a French physiologist (1813 - 1878), "The living being does not form an exception to the great natural harmony which makes things adapt themselves to one another; it breaks no concord; it is neither in contradiction to, nor struggling against, general cosmic forces. Far from that, it is a member of the universal concept of things, and the life of the animal, for example, is only a fragment of the total life of the universe." Huxley takes note of the "great natural harmony" to emphasize that man has succeeded in creating only disharmony.

POINT COUNTER POINT

TEXTUAL ANALYSIS

CHAPTER ONE

The novel, set in London, opens with Walter Bidlake telling his mistress, Marjorie Carling, he has an engagement for the evening. She implores him to come home early, and he leaves to attend a party and see Lucy Tantamount, his latest love interest.

Marjorie had left her husband two years before to live with Walter, and now she is expecting a child. Although Marjorie is still devoted to him, Walter remains with her from a sense of duty, not love. He is twenty-four now, and she is a few years older. At first he considered their relationship an idyllic one; now he finds it boring and frustrating. Marjorie still loves Walter but is hurt and upset by his lack of interest in her.

Comment

The two characters are drawn with great care; Walter - young, proud, disillusioned with his present life, his romantic ideas about love and life now destroyed; Marjorie - kind, devoted, frustrated by Walter's attitude towards her, her dream of love and life now destroyed. A few years together had turned their dream world into a world of boredom and frustration.

Huxley's comments on the fetus growing in Marjorie's womb bring together vividly the physical and spiritual elements in man: this tiny lump will become a human being who loves and hates, suffers and enjoys, creates and destroys. This lump, this man, has the potential for good and evil - for right and wrong.

POINT COUNTER POINT

TEXTUAL ANALYSIS

CHAPTER TWO

The musical party at Tantamount House is presided over by Lady Edward Tantamount, nee Hilda Sutton. (Hilda was twenty-five and Edward was forty when she encouraged the millionaire biologist to woo and wed her.) During the concert Lady Edward is seated next to John Bidlake, Walter's father, a painter of some distinction, and her sometimes lover.

Comment

We see a pattern developing now - the illicit love of Walter and Marjorie repeated by John Bidlake and Lady Edward; the affair hinted at between Walter and Lucy Tantamount, Lady Edward's daughter, providing still another variation of this theme.

POINT COUNTER POINT

TEXTUAL ANALYSIS

CHAPTER THREE

Meanwhile, Lord Edward Tantamount is continuing his biological research with his laboratory assistant, Frank Illidge. Hearing the music, they descend the main staircase, making an absurd entrance into the glittering crowd which is formally dressed for the concert.

Comment

Lord Edward - wealthy, aristocratic, brilliant - contrasts sharply with the characters we have met thus far. While still as young man, Lord Edward had found inspiration in the words of Claude Bernard, a French physiologist, "The living being ... is a member of the universal concert of things." Through his experiments and research he sought to prove and illustrate this idea.

POINT COUNTER POINT

TEXTUAL ANALYSIS

CHAPTER FOUR

....

The guests slily discuss Lord and Lady Edward's eccentricities; however, much is forgiven them because of their wealth and position. Illidge is introduced to Everard Webley, the founder and leader of the Brotherhood of British Freemen, a radical political group which advocates the abolition of majority rule and recognition of the superiority of particular individuals.

Comment

Lady Edward has few friends because she uses them as the butt of her practical jokes; she is tolerated because of her position and power. Lucy, her daughter, in many ways echoes her mother's sentiments, ideas, and characteristics.

POINT COUNTER POINT

TEXTUAL ANALYSIS

CHAPTER FIVE

The guests form little cliques and talk flatteringly about each other or themselves. Walter and Illidge discuss the people at the party; Illidge's disgust with and hatred of the wealthy class is manifest. Everard Webley attempts to win Lord Edward's support for his cause; Lord Edward, however, is interested only in things of the mind and the spirit. Denis Burlap, editor of the Literary World and Walter's employer, discusses his virtue and spirituality with anyone who will listen (Meanwhile Marjorie re-reads Walter's letters and recalls their life together.)

Comment

Lord Edward's honesty, sincerity, dedication, and self-satisfaction, emphasize the dishonesty, insincerity, vacillation, and self-recrimination apparent in the others. (Huxley provides strong, contrasting characters to act as stabilizing elements in his composition.) But Huxley does not present Lord Edward as an admirable character since he was "in all but intellect a child."

POINT COUNTER POINT

TEXTUAL ANALYSIS

CHAPTERS SIX AND SEVEN

CHAPTER SIX

Elinor Quarles, John Bidlake's daughter, and her husband, Philip, are about to leave India to return to London. For ten months they have been traveling throughout the East to find material for his novels and to find themselves. Philip is intellectual, aloof, solitary; Elinor is sociable outgoing warm-hearted - consequently their relationship is often strained.

CHAPTER SEVEN

Before leaving the party to meet some of her friends, Walter and Lucy stop to chat with General Knowles. Aware of the animosity between the General and his stepson, Maurice Spandrell, she extols the son to see how the general will react. Like her mother, Lucy enjoys experimenting with people's emotions.

Comment

Both Lucy and Lady Edward enjoy putting people in embarrassing situations to see their reactions. This gives them a sense of power, a sense of control.

Meanwhile, Molly d'Evergillod, a "professional' conversationalist, and Denis Burlap are discussing Philip Quarles. Molly remarks that Elinor is not intelligent and stimulating enough for Philip; she feels she could better satisfy his intellectual needs.

POINT COUNTER POINT

TEXTUAL ANALYSIS

CHAPTERS EIGHT AND NINE

CHAPTER EIGHT

Waiting at the restaurant for Lucy and Walter are Mark and Mary Rampion, and Maurice Spandrell; they are discussing the virtues of a happy marriage. Mark and Mary have been happily married for more than fifteen years; Spandrell, a bachelor, uses love to corrupt and hurt others, and himself.

CHAPTER NINE

Mary recalls when she first met Mark; Mary was then twenty-two and Mark a year younger. Their social backgrounds were quite different - Mary from a wealthy family and Mark from a poor one - but they found happiness in compromise and understanding.

Comment

Mark and Mary's harmonious life contrasts vividly with the life of deception, hypocrisy, and insincerity led by the others. Like Sir Edward, they act as stabilizing elements in the composition. Mark and Mary are patterned after Huxley's friends, D. H. Lawrence (the novelist) and his wife, Frieda.

POINT COUNTER POINT

TEXTUAL ANALYSIS

CHAPTERS TEN AND ELEVEN

CHAPTER TEN

Spandrell proudly boasts of his female conquests, generalizing from a single pitiful affair. Mark views this civilized promiscuity as absurd and shameful; he feels man should strike a balance between the physical and spiritual and accept both.

Comment

Mark recalls the Greek ideal of accepting man as both a spiritual and physical being. He considers modern morality based on Christianity and the demands of big business demoralizing and dehumanizing - to deny the physical or the spiritual is to deny a part of man.

CHAPTER ELEVEN

Walter wants to be alone with Lucy, but at her insistence they join the group at Sbisa's Restaurant. The discussion turns to Beatrice Gilroy, who works with Walter on the staff of the Literary World.

Comment

Beatrice idolizes Denis Burlap - she donates her services to the magazine; she rents him the upper floor of her house; she cares for him like a "mother." Beatrice trusts Denis - she thinks he is good, and kind, and the epitome of virtue. Unbeknown to her, he uses his spirituality and virtue as aids to seduce the innocent.

Continuing the musical analogy, Huxley brings together several variations on the same **theme** in the several characters - each viewing love in life differently; Lucy views love as a game, and toys with Walter's emotions; Mary and Mark Rampion have found love in married bliss; Beatrice desires a spiritual love; Denis flaunts a love of the spirit to cloak his lust; Lord Edward loves the wonders of nature; John Bidlake loves the passion and exuberance of life. Our symphonic view of life continues - new instruments are introduced, certain moods are repeated, the **theme** is varied - but the melody lingers on.

POINT COUNTER POINT

TEXTUAL ANALYSIS

CHAPTERS TWELVE AND THIRTEEN

CHAPTER TWELVE

At 1:30 a.m. Lucy and Walter leave the restaurant with Spandrell, who takes them to meet some of his Communist friends; one of them is Illidge. Finally Walter leaves to return to Marjorie, who has been sorrowfully awaiting his return. Spandrell and Lucy go to her home; they discuss her relationship with Walter. Spandrell is at one and the same time amused and bemused by her attitude towards Walter; having once been her lover, he is curious about her new affair.

CHAPTER THIRTEEN

By the next morning Walter had made three resolutions: he would never see Lucy again; he would spend every evening with Marjorie; he would ask Burlap for more money. By nightfall his good resolutions had come to nought.

Comment

Walter is a weak-willed individual who is unable or unwilling to face reality - his romance with Marjorie was based on romantic illusions; he is unable to resist Lucy's machinations; Burlap manipulates him at will.

Having cunningly dismissed Walter's request for a pay increase, Burlap dictates several letters to his secretary, Miss Cobbett. Ethel Cobbett had been a childhood friend of the late Mrs. Burlap. She had been impressed by his devotion to his wife's memory, and he had persuaded her to come to London to be his secretary.

Comment

Burlap is, perhaps, the most despicable character in the novel - he is a lecherous hypocrite who flaunts virtue in the pursuit of vice.

As Spandrell waits for his mother to arrive with some money, the bitter memory returns - his mother had remarried when he was fifteen, and he had never forgiven her. He takes his revenge by blaming her for his immoral, indifferent ways, and she, accepting the blame, continues to support him.

Comment

Still another variation is added - Freud would call it an Oedipus complex (the sexual attraction felt by the son for his mother).

POINT COUNTER POINT

TEXTUAL ANALYSIS

CHAPTER FOURTEEN

While Elinor and Philip traveled through the East, little Phil, their son, remained with his grandmother and with his nurse, Miss Fulkes.

Comment

John Bidlake had married Janet Poston (his third wife) when he was ill and needed companionship; when he recovered he returned to his lusty former life. For twenty-five years he had come and gone at will; Mrs. Bidlake found consolation in mysticism and endless meditation.

While returning from Bombay, Philip and Elinor discuss Walter's relationship with Marjorie. Philip feels that Walter cannot cope with the realities of life - he looks for an ideal love but finds only boredom.

> Comment

Having discussed Walter and Marjorie's situation, Philip remarks how people look at the same thing but see it differently. As a novelist he wants to look at something and see all its different aspects at once. This, of course, is what Huxley is attempting in *Point Counter Point*.

POINT COUNTER POINT

TEXTUAL ANALYSIS

CHAPTER FIFTEEN

Walter and Marjorie continue deluding themselves and each other - she considers leaving him but realizes she has nowhere to go. Walter spurns her love even as Lucy spurns his.

Comment

Another pattern repeated - Marjorie loves Walter, but he feels little affection for her; Walter loves Lucy, but she refuses to love him.

POINT COUNTER POINT

TEXTUAL ANALYSIS

CHAPTER SIXTEEN

Burlap visits the Rampions in Chelsea. Mary detests him as a "spiritual leech," but Mark rather enjoys his company. The two men discuss the life of St. Francis that Burlap is writing; Mark proceeds to taunt Burlap with parodies of the lives of the saint. That evening Burlap recounts the day's experiences to Beatrice.

Comment

Mark recognizes the **irony** of Burlap writing about the life of St. Francis. He knows that Burlap flaunts his supposed virtue and piety to more easily win the confidence of the virtuous female; then he seduces her. Note the skill with which Burlap is encouraging Beatrice's confidence.

POINT COUNTER POINT

TEXTUAL ANALYSIS

CHAPTER SEVENTEEN

While drinking at the bar one day, Spandrell falls into conversation with one of the habitués - it is Marjorie's husband. Being somewhat drunk, as usual, he tells Spandrell about his wife leaving him and about his work - he is writing the lives of the English saints, in verse. Later Spandrell tells Walter and Lucy of the encounter.

Comment

This juxtaposition of virtue and vice repeats itself - the drunkard writes religious verse; the lustful Burlap writes of the saintly Francis.

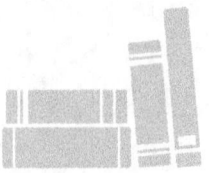

POINT COUNTER POINT

TEXTUAL ANALYSIS

CHAPTER EIGHTEEN

A "Romola Saville" had sent some passionate love poetry to the Literary World, and, as was his custom with women contributors, Burlap invites her to stop by. Much to his distress, "Romola Saville" was the pseudonym used by two elderly women; Burlap soon dismisses them.

That evening Beatrice helps "doctor" Burlap's cold - she fixes hot milk and honey and rubs his chest with camphorated oil. Little by little Burlap gains her confidence, and she enjoys the intimacy occasioned by these ministrations.

Comment

Although Miss Cobbett warns her about Burlap's reputation, Beatrice is unable to think ill of him.

POINT COUNTER POINT

TEXTUAL ANALYSIS

CHAPTERS NINETEEN AND TWENTY

CHAPTERS NINETEEN

Philip and Elinor arrive home amid great confusion and good cheer. That night, Philip records his impression of the day's events; he sees each person, each event, each thing as part of a universal continuum.

Comment

Philip is afraid of losing his freedom; he sees in his family (Elinor and little Phil) a threat to this freedom. At one and the same time he is attracted and repulsed by this situation.

CHAPTER TWENTY

Philip Quarles' mother and father are a study in contrasts: Rachel is intelligent, tactful, efficient, understanding; Sidney is arrogant, indolent, self-centered, superficially clever. Rachel spends her whole life tactfully smoothing over the damage he does and encouraging him in each new interest - business, politics, writing.

Comment

Sidney Quarles is one of Huxley's more humorous characters - his affected speech and manner, his concern with appearances, and his patronizing attitude make him a ridiculous spectacle.

Mr. Quarles' latest project - a history of democracy - necessitates many trips to London. However, most of his "research" is concerned with Gladys, his latest combination secretary-mistress.

POINT COUNTER POINT

TEXTUAL ANALYSIS

CHAPTER TWENTY - ONE

Elinor and Philip decide to visit old friends - Elinor goes to Everard's apartment, and Philip goes to his club.

Comment

Sometime before, Everard had declared his love to Elinor; she found him attractive but did not encourage him. Everard renews his protestations of love, but Elinor remains adamant.

At the club Philip meets Spandrell, Illidge, and Walter. The discussion turns to the forces that shape men's lives - Illidge calls it chance; Spandrell says things happen to suit the individual; Philip believes each individual interprets an event in his own way; Walter expresses no opinion.

Comment

Huxley presents three views of life - life as chance, life as a manifestation of divine providence, life as a self-directed, self-interpreted existence.

That evening Elinor tells Philip that Everard is in love with her; Philip considers the idea quite amusing.

Comment

Philip is completely self-sufficient and refuses allegiance to any person or thing; Elinor hopes to jolt him by her confession. Philip refuses to be concerned.

POINT COUNTER POINT

TEXTUAL ANALYSIS

CHAPTER TWENTY - TWO

Philip jots ideas for a novel in his notebook - he will select a theme and develop many variations and parallel plots; each character will personify a particular idea or belief; many of the characters will be novelists who can offer different views.

Comment

With tongue in cheek Huxley tells the reader what his belief that the individual must be aware of his human - developed many variations, related characters and situations, offered many points of view. He has created characters who illustrate particular beliefs and ideas. He has included numerous writers - Walter, Philip, Mark, Denis, and Sidney Quarles.

POINT COUNTER POINT

TEXTUAL ANALYSIS

CHAPTERS TWENTY - THREE AND TWENTY - FOUR

CHAPTER TWENTY - THREE

Mark Rampion believes that any concern with political ideologies is absurd; he tells Philip he believes that humanity's salvation lies in the individual's recognition of his own humanity.

Comment

Huxley, in the person of Mark Rampion, restates his belief that the individual must be aware of his humanness, of his individuality, if mankind is to survive.

CHAPTER TWENTY - FOUR

Meanwhile, others have their own concerns: Mr. Quarles has been continuing his "research" with Gladys, although she mocks his pretensions and cheapness; Philip has found his role as father tedious; John Bidlake has developed a tumor.

POINT COUNTER POINT

TEXTUAL ANALYSIS

CHAPTERS TWENTY - FIVE AND TWENTY - SIX

CHAPTER TWENTY - FIVE

Lucy writes to Walter from Paris, where she has gone for a change of scenery. Soon bored, she suggests he meet her in Madrid; just as quickly she changes her mind and decides to remain in Paris.

CHAPTER TWENTY - SIX

Philip writes his impressions of Mark Rampion in his notebook - he admires him because he is realistic and accepts life for what it is.

Comment

Philip's association with Mark has taught him that the search for Truth is but an attempt to deny the reality of one's own existence. Like many people, Philip has sought an intellectual life in order to avoid confronting life itself - the part is substituted for the whole.

POINT COUNTER POINT

TEXTUAL ANALYSIS

CHAPTERS TWENTY - SEVEN AND TWENTY - EIGHT

CHAPTER TWENTY - SEVEN

John Bidlake, sick and dejected, goes back to Gattenden and Mrs. Bidlake. As in years past, he returns because of illness.

CHAPTER TWENTY - EIGHT

Philip has gone to see Molly d'Evergillod and they talk of love in life. Philip becomes amorous, but Molly protests; she thinks love should be platonic and intellectual.

Comment

Poor Philip - for years he has avoided any such emotional entanglement; now, for a change, he is the one repulsed.

On the way home Philip decides to tell Elinor of his escapade. A certain animosity has separated them of late, and he hopes to be reconciled with Elinor. Although Elinor wants the reconciliation as much as Philip does, she wants to punish him for his former aloofness.

Comment

Philip and Elinor want to change but have difficulty doing so. They have established patterns of behavior which are not easily changed.

POINT COUNTER POINT

TEXTUAL ANALYSIS

CHAPTER TWENTY - NINE

Everard Webley, on a white horse and with a sword at his side, addresses the British Freemen at a rally in Hyde Park. Elinor is present and is thrilled and elated by his stirring speech extolling the virtues of his Freeman. Illidge heckles him, is pounced upon and beaten, and then hustled from the scene.

Comment

Elinor is exhilarated by Everard's address; Illidge is irritated. Elinor sees Everard as a romantic idol; Illidge sees him as a tool of the rich.

Illidge meets Spandrell and recounts his adventure - he is proud of his action. Spandrell laughs at Illidge's feeble protest and tells him he should take more direct action - perhaps murder Everard.

The next day Elinor and Everard drive through the countryside; Elinor finds herself drawn to Everard, hesitates, and then yields to his kisses. Nearby, Spandrell and Connie, an aging prostitute, are walking among the flowers. He has brought her there for the pleasure of humiliating and hurting her.

Comment

The juxtaposition of the two couples provides variation on a theme. Elinor is attracted and repulsed by Everard's sense of power; Spandrell is attracted and repulsed by Connie's personification of lust.

POINT COUNTER POINT

TEXTUAL ANALYSIS

CHAPTERS THIRTY AND THIRTY - ONE

CHAPTER THIRTY

Rachel Quarles visits Marjorie - she feels sorry for her in her predicament and becomes her friend and confidante. With Rachel's help Marjorie finds peace and happiness in God.

Walter, humiliated and disappointed when Lucy changes her mind about meeting him in Madrid, sends her a letter of reproach. Lucy replies that what she does is her own business - to "punish" him she tells about her latest amorous fling.

CHAPTER THIRTY - ONE

Much to Sidney Quarles' dismay, Gladys arrives at the house and announces she is expecting a baby. Mrs. Quarles, no longer surprised at anything he does, comes to his rescue.

POINT COUNTER POINT

TEXTUAL ANALYSIS

CHAPTERS THIRTY - TWO AND THIRTY - THREE

CHAPTER THIRTY - TWO

Elinor realizes that she must choose between Philip and Everard that night - Everard is coming to the house at six o'clock. About four o'clock, Spandrell stops by to see Philip; before he leaves a telegram arrives - little Phil is sick. Elinor asks Spandrell to call Everard and tell him not to come by; she must leave immediately.

Meanwhile Mrs. Quarles has called Philip and told him about his father's affair with Gladys. Philip arrives at the house and finds his father in bed with his dictaphone - before he dies he wants to record his philosophic musings for posterity.

CHAPTER THIRTY - THREE

Spandrell does not call Everard; he calls Illidge instead. They hide in the house and await Everard's arrival - when he arrives they pounce upon him and smash his skull.

Comment

The aftermath of the murder presents an interesting contrast - Spandrell is unconcerned, unfeeling, pleased with himself; Illidge is horrified and almost ill. The motivation for the murder provides still another contrast - Spandrell is not concerned with political ideology the way Illidge is; he simply wants to exert an influence for evil.

In the presence of this death, Huxley comments on life. (Recall the comments made regarding the fetus in Marjorie's womb.) Millions of cells unite to form the human body; at death they are absorbed into the surrounding world. This man, Everard Webley, his ambition, thoughts, emotions, likes and dislikes, love, and lust are gone - "a fragment of the total life of the universe."

They place Webley's body in the back of his own car; Spandrell takes Illidge to Tantamount House, parks the car in a crowded section of town, and then takes a bus to Sbisa's Restaurant to see Philip.

POINT COUNTER POINT

TEXTUAL ANALYSIS

CHAPTER THIRTY - FOUR

Philip, Burlap, Rampion, and Spandrell discuss the ideas and beliefs that mold a man's mind - Rampion dominates the discussion. He believes that man has been perverted by religion, science and education; the truth of one's existence is discovered only by living completely, accepting the whole man - mental and physical.

Comment

Huxley uses Mark Rampion as his mouthpiece to state some of his own beliefs. Huxley believes that the proper study of Mankind if Man - Man as an individual and Man as a member of the human race.

Burlap returns home; Beatrice has waited up for him, as usual. She sits on his bed with his head in her lap and strokes his forehead - she thinks of him as a little boy. Softly and patiently he caresses her; finally she yields to him.

Comment

The spiritual and physical intermingled are interchanged - an ironic and perverted manifestation of Rampion's idea.

POINT COUNTER POINT

TEXTUAL ANALYSIS

CHAPTER THIRTY - FIVE

....

Philip arrives at Gattenden and learns that little Phil has meningitis. The newspapers arrive with the announcement of Everard's murder; Elinor almost faints at the news.

Each day John Bidlake inquires after the condition of his grandson but he refuses to go near him. He sees the boy as himself - he does not want to be reminded of pain and death. A little later the child dies.

Comment

John Bidlake's seeing himself in little Phil is another instance where Huxley uses a multiple image - putting characters in similar situations to see how they will react.

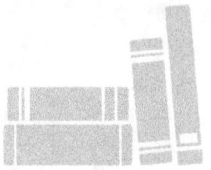

POINT COUNTER POINT

TEXTUAL ANALYSIS

CHAPTERS THIRTY - SIX AND THIRTY - SEVEN

CHAPTER THIRTY - SIX

Since the police have no clues to the murder of Everard Webley, Spandrell ponders his next move. When he meets Philip he expresses his sympathy; Philip is embarrassed; he does not want anyone to see his misery.

CHAPTER THIRTY - SEVEN

Spandrell believes he has found proof of God's existence in the music of Beethoven - the interweaving of the melody duplicating the interweaving of men's lives.

Comment

Huxley again uses music to highlight the action and to complete the cycle begun at Lady Edward's musical party.

Spandrell invites Mark and Mary Rampion to share his discovery, arranging beforehand his own grand finale.

Comment

Once Spandrell felt he had found the truth, he notified the British Freemen where the murderer could be found. Then while Mark and Mary listen to the phonograph, he walks out of the room and is shot.

Burlap whistles as he walks home - he has sold the serial rights to his life of St. Francis, he has been invited to give a series of lectures on ethics, and he has gotten rid of Miss Cobbett.

That night he and Beatrice romp in the bathtub together like little children - "of such is the kingdom of heaven."

POINT COUNTER POINT

CHARACTER ANALYSES

Marjorie Carling

An earnest, cultured young woman, she left her husband to become Walter Bidlake's mistress.

Walter Bidlake

A weak-willed, romantic young man, he works as a staff writer for the Literary World.

Lady Edward Tantamount

A woman who uses her charm and wit to obtain position and power.

Lord Edward Tantamount

A man of wealth, title, and intellect, his feelings, intuitions, and instincts are those of a little boy.

John Bidlake

A painter of some renown, he spends his life in lusty pursuits. He is the father of Walter and Elinor.

Elinor Bidlake Quarles

An intelligent, attractive, devoted wife, she is frustrated by her husband's aloofness.

Philip Quarles

An aspiring novelist, he refuses allegiance to anybody or anything - except on his own terms.

Lucy Tantamount

The willful daughter of Lord and Lady Tantamount, she inherited his intelligence and her playfulness and employs both for her own pleasures.

Alfred Illidge

Lord Edward's laboratory assistant embraces communism as a concrete expression of his own hatred of the rich and powerful.

Everard Webley

He is the founder and head of the Brotherhood of British Freemen, a group which advocates many of the Nazi Party principles.

Denis Burlap

The lustful editor of the Literary World writes of ethical and religious matters.

Mary And Mark Rampion

Although they express radical ideas about love and morality, their married life is exemplary in every way.

Maurice Spandrell

The dissolute stepson of General Knowles, he spends his life seeking to do evil.

Mrs. Knowles

Maurice's widowed mother remarried when he was fifteen - he never forgives her and blames her for his wasted life.

Miss Ethel Cobbett

A childhood friend of the late Mrs. Burlap, she moves to London to become Denis' secretary.

Beatrice Gilroy

Afraid of men because of a traumatic experience when quite young, she "adores" Denis Burlap because he is so trustworthy and spiritual.

Sidney Quarles

Although success has always eluded Philip's father, his own high opinion of himself has sustained him.

Rachel Quarles

Relying on her own intelligence, ingenuity, and tact, she finds peace of mind in spite of her unfortunate marriage to Sidney.

POINT COUNTER POINT

ESSAY QUESTIONS AND ANSWERS

....

Question: Discuss the significance of D. H. Lawrence's remark to Huxley about *Point Counter Point* - "I do think you've shown the truth ... about you and your generation, with really fine courage."

Answer: The truth that Huxley has shown in this novel is the tendency of an individual to devote himself exclusively to a particular idea or ideal which might be considered good, bad, or indifferent. With the exception of the Rampions, each character in the novel is one-sided and, consequently, is not a complete person. In the words of Mark Rampion, "Civilization is harmony and completeness. Reason, feeling, instinct, the life of the body .... Barbarism is being lopsided. You can be a barbarian of the intellect as well as of the body." In this novel most of the characters are concerned with but a single aspect of their humanity-seeking sensual pleasure, dedicating self to an ideal, pursuing intellectual matters. Because Huxley's readers might well recognize that they themselves are "barbarians," courage is an appropriate noun.

Question: Discuss the importance of Philip Quarles' *Notebook*.

Answer: Huxley commented that Philip Quarles is "in part a portrait of me"; consequently Philip's comments concerning the novel he would like to write might well be applied to Huxley's work. In chapter twenty-two, Philip makes several notes regarding the novel he would like to write; these notes in turn describe Huxley's novel. For instance, he talks about the use of parallel themes, the value of showing the various aspects of a single event, the possibilities offered by putting a novelist into the novel. In chapter twenty-six, Philip's musings regarding Rampion's ideas might well be Huxley's thoughts about D. H. Lawrence's ideas; Philip speaks of his admiration for Mark because "he lives in a more satisfactory way than anyone I know." Philip also regards his own "Search for Truth" an elaborate substitute for genuine living. A close reading of the *Notebook* entries provides a thumbnail sketch of *Point Counter Point*, many insights into Huxley's beliefs and concerns at the time he wrote the novel, and some interesting comments on the "novel of ideas."

Question: Why does *Point Counter Point* lack a "satisfying conclusion"? Why is nothing neally resolved?

Answer: Recalling Mark Rampion's words, "Civilization is harmony and completeness," the lack of harmony and completeness in the novel itself emphasizes the barbarism of the people and the times (the Rampions excepted). At the end of the novel, the reader might ask, "Then what happened?" But there is no satisfactory answer because nothing happened. Huxley was disillusioned and disgusted with mankind and held little hope for its ultimate redemption. Because what man does is meaningless and because what happens to man is meaningless, the ending of the novel expresses the meaninglessness of life-Beatrice and Burlap romping in the bathtub.

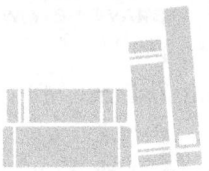

AFTER MANY A SUMMER DIES THE SWAN

INTRODUCTION

This novel might well be called Huxley's Hollywood novel since we may use the same adjectives to describe the novel that we would use to describe Hollywood, its people, and its productions - extravagant, preposterous, outrageous, unbelievable. (These adjectives were even more applicable in 1938, when the novel was written, than today.) Huxley lived in California for many years and wrote movie scenarios, and his novel caricatures the life and the people he knew there. *After Many a Summer* attempts to outdo Hollywood in making the extraordinary, ordinary; the unbelievable, believable; and the impossible, possible.

In the novel Jeremy Pordage, a visiting English scholar, is amazed at what he sees when he first arrives in California. We might well suspect that Huxley himself reacted with a like degree of amazement and disbelief. Because truth is stranger than fiction and because there is a reality in fiction even as there is a fiction in reality, the characters and the situations in this novel are at one and the same time real and imaginary. The multimillionaire, the starlets, the castle, the migrant workers, the cemetery - they are all in California and they are all in this novel.

The novel is a comedy - the story of one man's search for the secret of longevity. The outlandish characters, the fabulous setting, and the comical situations contribute to the sensationalism of the plot. But Mr. Propter's preaching detracts from the story; *After Many a Summer* proves again Huxley's preoccupation with ideas to the detriment of the novel as a novel. Nevertheless, it is Mr. Propter who "says" what Huxley wants to say.

As noted earlier, Huxley often uses a spokesman for his ideas and his beliefs. Often the spokesman is a minor character - in *After Many a Summer* Huxley's spokesman (Mr. Propter) is the main character. In chapter nine, Mr. Propter expresses Huxley's ideas about where "good" is: "On the lower level, good exists as the proper functioning of the organism in accordance with the laws of its own being. On the higher level, it exists in the form of a knowledge of the world without desire or aversion; it exists as the experience of eternity, as the transcendence of personality, the extension of consciousness beyond the limits imposed by the ego." This is basically what Huxley wanted to say - the novel is simply the "message carrier."

AFTER MANY A SUMMER DIES THE SWAN

TEXTUAL ANALYSIS

PART ONE

....

CHAPTER ONE

Upon his arrival in California, Jeremy Pordage is met by Mr. Stoyte's chauffeur. During the drive from the station the chauffeur points out the advertisements for a number of Mr. Stoyte's very successful ventures - oil, banking, and even a cemetery. Reading the billboards amuses Jeremy-Classy Eats. Jesus Saves. Hamburgers. Beverly Pantheon, the Cemetery That Is Different; having been in American but a week, he still finds many things amazing and amusing.

Comment

Huxley uses the ride from the station to Mr. Stoyte's castle to provide a study in contrasts - the slums and the mansions, the rich and the poor, the white and the colored, the comic and the pathetic. The billboards reflect these contrasts with their advertisement for God and gum, for bras and business, for finance and funerals, for sandwiches and salvation - God and Mammon together in the marketplace. This study in contrasts continues throughout the novel since there are conflicts not only between ideologies, between social classes, and between individuals, but also conflicts within the individual himself.

Jeremy asks the chauffeur to stop a moment so that he can cable his mother. Though fifty-four years old he still acknowledges her maternal domination. It is an expensive message, but the cost is no object of concern; Mr. Stoyte is paying him six thousand dollars for three month's work.

Comment

Jeremy Pordage is English by nationality, research scholar by inclination and training, and mother - dominated by choice. He has been hired by Mr. Stoyte to sort out and catalogue the Hauberk Papers, an historically important collection of British documents.

CHAPTER TWO

The chauffeur takes Jeremy on a tour of the Beverly Pantheon, the Personality Cemetery, one of Mr. Stoyte's most profitable holdings. The reproductions of famous buildings, the landscaping, the nude statues of beautiful females, the fountains, the piped - in music, the statues of the Infant Jesus and Peter Pan - Jeremy sees it all, but still can't believe it is real.

> Comment

This is California - where the impossible is possible, the unreal becomes real, where everything is stupendous, colossal, and magnificent. Huxley's description of the Beverly Pantheon is based in part, at least, on California's most famous cemetery, Forest Lawn.

Nearing the castle Mr. Stoyte had built as his symbol of success, the chauffeur stops to pick up Mr. Propter, and Jeremy learns that Mr. Propter and Jo Stoyte had been classmates some fifty years before. Mr. Propter explains that Jo Stoyte, who had been, called Slob or Jelly-Belly at school, is now overcompensating for his glandular deficiencies. Leaving Mr. Propter at his cottage, they cross the moat and arrive at the castle's main entrance; a small, thick-set man rushes out to greet Jeremy - it is Mr. Stoyte.

> Comment

Jeremy is immediately impressed with Mr. Propter and his apparent intelligence, sensibility, serenity, energy, and strength. The comment about old Jelly-Belly he sees immediately manifested in the castle and in the demeanor of its owner. Mr. Stoyte wants everyone to know that he's a self-made man - he can buy what he wants, people and culture included.

CHAPTER THREE

Mr. Stoyte's tour of the estate makes Jeremy aware of two of the multimillionaire's latest interests - the Stoyte Home for Sick Children, where he plays the role of the benevolent father, and the boudoir of Miss Maunciple, a young lady friend, where he plays. When they leave the Home, Mr. Stoyte is terribly upset by the presence of a strange car (he fears kidnappers) and begins to scream at those responsible for its presence there. Suddenly he remembers Dr. Obispo's warning after his first stroke and swallows his anger.

Comment

Mr. Stoyte likes to be referred to as "Uncle Jo" by the children at the Home and by Miss Maunciple. As part of the overcompensation mentioned by Mr. Propter, he enjoys the role of benefactor - both the children and Miss Maunciple "adore" him because of his generous nature. Of course Jelly-Belly never does something for nothing; his generosity provides him with mental and physical satisfaction.

In this moment of crisis when he feels he must control his temper, Mr. Stoyte repeats the words of his dead wife who had been a Christian Scientist, "God is love. There is no death." Fearing death, he wants to believe these words, but as often as not he also remembers the text that had hung over his cot during his youth: "It is a terrible thing to fall into the hands of the living God." Mr. Stoyte fears death, any thought or any reminder of it; even a visit to the offices of the Beverly Pantheon distresses him.

Comment

His fear of death, his desire to avoid any thought of death, and his attempts to outwit death have become an obsession with Mr. Stoyte. His support of the research on longevity carried on by his personal physician and his affair with Miss Maunciple are manifestations of this obsession.

CHAPTER FIVE

Jeremy begins his work on the Hauberk Papers, which had been purchased from two old spinster ladies who were the last of a once proud line of barons and earls. While gloating over his treasure - "these delicious fragments of English history" - he hears a knock at the door. Dr. Obispo, Mr. Stoyte's personal physician, bursts into the room, make irreverent remarks about their employer, shows his happy derision of everybody, and invites Jeremy to see his laboratory. Jeremy would like to protest this intrusion but, as usual, says nothing.

Having introduced his young assistant, Peter Boone, the doctor explains some of his research, his experiments with mice and guinea pigs, the effects of hormone treatments, and his interest in the longevity of carp. (He had acquired some two-hundred-year-old carp which were perfectly healthy and showed no symptoms of senility.) Dr. Obispo feels that the secret of longevity lies in the peculiar bacteria inhabiting the carp's intestine; his experiments now center on isolating the organism responsible for the carp's immunity to old age. He thinks he might find something that would work on Uncle Jo.

CHAPTER SIX

At lunch with Mr. Stoyte that day are Jeremy, Dr. Obispo, Peter Boone, Virginia Maunciple, two of her women friends from Hollywood, and Dr. Herbert Mulge, the Principal of Tarzana College. The particular interests of each are apparent - Dr. Mulge discusses the possibility of an endowment from Mr. Stoyte; Peter alludes to his experiences during the Spanish Civil War; the doctor tells the girls dirty jokes; and Jeremy sits, thinks about all the things he should say, but says nothing.

Comment

Huxley's luncheon conversation provides some interesting contrasts and some wry humor. Dr. Mulge, Ph.D., D.D., uses all the persuasive means at his command to raise funds for Tarzana to make it the "Parthenon and Academe, the Stoa and the Temple of the Muses for the Los Angeles Metropolitan Area." And the possible source of these funds is Mr. Stoyte, the self-made man who doesn't know what a Stoa is and doesn't care. Pete Boone, the young idealist, with his enthusiasm for liberty and justice and his devotion to the cause of science, silently adores Virginia as the epitome of feminine virtue, goodness, and grace. For her part, Miss Maunciple adores her body for the pleasure it gives to her and others - pleasure is her ideal.

CHAPTER SEVEN

Lunch over, Jeremy returns to the wonderful treasure he had been forced to abandon temporarily. One of his exciting finds that afternoon is a pornographic work bound as a prayer book. Later that afternoon Virginia and Dr. Obispo stop by. Paging through the books that Jeremy has put aside, the doctor roars with laughter when he sees the "prayer book"; since it is in French, he promises Virginia he will translate it for her later.

The three leave together to meet Pete before they go down the hill to pay a call on Mr. Propter. They pass the baboon cage, a nymph which spouts water from her polished breasts, and the Grotto of the Queen of Heaven which Uncle Jo had built at Virginia's request. Suddenly Dr. Obispo remembers some letters he has to write, and a little later Virginia remarks how tired she feels; Jeremy and Pete are left to make the social call alone.

> Comment

Virginia's feelings and remarks about the love life of the baboon, the artistic portrayal of nudity, and the efficacy of prayer provide an interesting contrast in values. Virginia likes to watch the baboons copulate and exclaims, "Aren't they human!" Being of the age of bottle feeding and contraception, she is disgusted by the statue of the nymph because she finds the idea of motherhood revolting. The Grotto was constructed in thanksgiving for her relief from sinus trouble - a victory for the Queen of Heaven and for Virginia. Virginia is a little like the pornographic book disguised as the Book of Common Prayer.

CHAPTER EIGHT

Mr. Propter sits meditating on "What is Man?" He considers one possible answer to the question: A nothingness surrounded by God; indigent and capable of God, filled with God if he so desires. Mr. Propter believes that man may experience timeless good, be "filled with God," if he has good will, intelligence, and the willingness to free himself from himself.

> Comment

Huxley believed that since man was composed of body and soul, of the animal and the spirit, of the hands and the mind, he should accept and use his two-sided humanity. In his essay "Vulgarity in Literature," published in 1931, Huxley states: "I think it not only permissible but necessary, that literature should take cognizance of physiology and should investigate the still obscure relations between the mind and its body." Mr. Propter is concerned with the mind and its body. His ideas are amplified and clarified in Mr. Propter's conversation with Pete and Jeremy.

With the arrival of Jeremy and Pete the conversation first turns to Jo and then to the experiments Pete and Dr. Obispo are conducting. Mr. Propter asks whether the prolongation of life might result in the species reverting to an earlier stage in the evolutionary process. Peter laughs, shrugs his shoulders, and says they would have to wait and see. At this point Mr. Propter brings up the subject of timeless good, his belief that man can be "filled with God." Jeremy is irritated by the turn the conversation has taken; he considers his life rational and civilized-meals on time, a daily walk, good books, the weekly journey to London, and, every alternate week, a visit to a trollop's flat.

Comment

Jeremy's view of a rational, civilized life provides a humorous contrast to Mr. Propter's view. Both men are well educated, scholarly, recognized authorities in their respective fields - Huxley notes these similarities in order to better contrast their respective views of the meaning, purpose, and value of life.

CHAPTER NINE

The conversation continues with Mr. Propter explaining his views of "timeless good" - the union of man with God. He believes that since God is Eternal Goodness, whatever is finite is potentially or actually evil. Man being finite achieves timeless good if he achieves union with God - is "filled with God." The first step must be man's liberation from time, from craving, from personality - his liberation into union with God. Mr. Propter believes that democratic institutions can aid the individual's achievement of timeless god by their respect for personality.

> Comment

Huxley uses Mr. Propter to explain his own philosophy and his own beliefs - his own disillusionment with scientists and artists whose work imprisons rather than liberates mankind. Many of Huxley's works satirize the scientist, the artist, the humanitarian, and the educator because Huxley felt that these people had betrayed mankind by creating and maintaining a society unworthy of mankind.

Pete asks how man should act, what man should do. Mr. Propter replies that man must discover what appropriate action should and must be taken. He explains that on the strictly human level of time and craving, man cannot achieve anything but evil and that man must fight for good where good is - on the level above and below the human level, on the spiritual level and on the animal level.

> Comment

The human level of time and craving refers to the world of "greed and fear and hatred, of war and capitalism and dictatorship and slavery - perpetual imprisonment of the ego." Mr. Propter explains that insofar as we are human beings we prevent ourselves from realizing the "physiological and instinctive good that we're capable of as animals" and "the spiritual and timeless good that we're capable of as potential inhabitants of eternity."

CHAPTER TEN

When Mr. Stoyte learns that Mr. Propter had reprimanded his estate manager for exploiting the migrant workers, he is furious. Although he admires Mr. Propter's intelligence, good will, and virtue, he resents him at the same time. Jo stops at Mr. Propter's place, upbraids him for interfering, and threatens to have him run out of the valley - but later he admits to himself that these are empty threats.

Arriving back at the castle, Jo immediately goes to Virginia's boudoir. Finding her with Dr. Obispo makes him suspicious and jealous, but they quickly allay his suspicions by their manifestations of concern for his health.

CHAPTER ELEVEN

After Mr. Stoyte's departure, Mr. Propter shows Jeremy and Pete some of his tools and gadgets. Since he wants to be independent - to keep the human activities from interfering too much with the manifestation of good on the other levels - he wants as far as possible to be self-sufficient. He tells them the world should develop a system that reduces the amount of fear, greed, hatred, and domineering to a minimum. And because he is practical, realistic, and intelligent, he admits that the realization of this system will be difficult if not impossible.

Comment

Huxley does not present Mr. Propter as a pessimistic prophet of doom or as an abstract theorizer. He is a practical person who lives his theories and practices what he preaches. He wants to make the world safe for man as animal and as spirit, and he considers self-sufficiency for himself and others the first step.

CHAPTER TWELVE

The three arrive at the castle and continue their discussion. Noting Mr. Stoyte's collection of painting and sculpture, Mr. Propter remarks that self-will may manifest itself in dedication to culture, in devotion to the irrelevancies of everyday life, or in the pursuit of a false ideal. According to Mr. Propter there are "a million wrong tracks and only one right - a million ideals, a million projections of personality, and only one God and one beatific vision." He speaks also of the inability of man to communicate because of the shortcomings of a given language and the ambiguity of a given word.

Comment

During Mr. Propter's explication of his philosophy Huxley keeps us aware of the others - Uncle Jo; Virginia, and Dr. Obispo. Their self-seeking and desire for self-gratification is alluded to throughout this section of the book - they illustrate Mr. Propter's remarks about "wrong tracks."

CHAPTER THIRTEEN

That night before going to sleep, Jeremy recalls the events of the day and decides that Mr. Propter is a kind of Ancient Mariner - but one that Jeremy cannot heed. In another room Pete is trying to figure things out - science and Mr. Propter, social justice and eternity, and Virginia and anti-Fascism. Virginia, meanwhile, is saying her prayers and painting her toenails - but these devotions are interrupted when Dr. Obispo enters her boudoir and seduces her.

AFTER MANY A SUMMER DIES THE SWAN

TEXTUAL ANALYSIS

PART TWO

CHAPTER ONE

Jeremy writes to his mother about recent events - Uncle Jo is glum and ill-tempered; Miss Maunciple has a dreamy, faraway look in her eyes; Dr. Obispo is continuing his research; and Mr. Propter has given up trying to edify him. Dominated by his mother, addicted to simple animal pleasures, self-satisfied with himself and his life - Jeremy sits, scratches himself, and picks at a scab as he meditates on life.

Comment

Part Two opens with a detailed psychological portrait of Jeremy, a scholar living on the fringe of life, whose intelligence and education has no effect on his personal life and beliefs.

Huxley was distressed by the inability and unwillingness of the intelligent and the educated to live thoughtful, reasonable, and worthwhile lives. Jeremy expresses the philosophy of the uncommitted and unconcerned intellectual when he says, "There was really no reason why one should do anything much about anything."

CHAPTER TWO

Virginia is unhappy and ashamed because she has betrayed Uncle Jo and Pete and Our Lady, in order to carry on her affair with Dr. Obispo. She wants to stop seeing him because when she thinks about what she is doing she feels bad; but she does it again because it stops her feeling bad about having done it before.

Comment

Huxley remarks in this chapter that men are continually trying "to lose their lives, the stale, unprofitable, senseless lives of their ordinary personalities" in a thousand different ways - gambling, religion, research, ambition, politics, sex, drugs, entertainment. Men escape the meaninglessness of life by attempting to escape the reality of life. Virginia finds her sexual relations with Dr. Obispo a means of escape.

CHAPTER THREE

Mr. Stoyte discusses some new plans for the Beverly Pantheon with the manager - these include a Poet's Corner for writers, and Catacombs. Although pleased with this possibility of making the cemetery even more popular and profitable, Jo cannot forget the disconcerting events of the past few weeks - he is feeling sluggish and out of sorts and Virginia is acting strange. He is sunk in a mood of perplexed and agitated gloom - his are the miseries of an old, tired, empty man.

Comment

Huxley continues his editorializing in this chapter - the plight of "the man who had no end in life but himself, no philosophy, no knowledge but of his own interests."

CHAPTER FOUR

Jeremy continues his work of unpacking, examining, and filing the Hauberk Papers; he turns now to the fifth earl's notebook. The old earl, like Jo Stoyte, had been concerned with power, pleasure, happiness, and the problem of old age. Like Dr. Obispo, the earl had wondered if the long-lived carp held the secret of eternal life. Jeremy found this similarity of ideas about longevity amusing.

CHAPTER FIVE

Peter remembers Virginia's attention to him during the last three weeks as both pleasurable and distressing - pleasurable because of his love for her innocence and goodness, but distressing because his belief in the Sacredness of Love causes him great anxiety. (Virginia feigns interest in Pete so Jo will not be suspicious of Dr. Obispo.) His conversations with Mr. Propter are another complicating factor because Pete now questions many things - the past and the future, good and evil, the actual and the fantastic, the beautiful and the ugly. He concludes that Mr. Propter is the only person he knows "who could make sense out of the absurd, insane, diabolical confusion of it all."

CHAPTER SIX

Jeremy tells Dr. Obispo about the fifth earl's notebook and offers to read sections of it for him. The earl had written about his eating the guts of the carp in the hope of finding the secret of longevity. The earl's comments indicate that these experiments seemed to have been at least partially successful.

CHAPTER SEVEN

Pete stops to visit Mr. Propter and helps him to make furniture for the migrant families. Their discussion today concerns optimism and pessimism. Mr. Propter explains that most people are optimistic about the wrong things (applied science and social reform) and pessimistic about the right things (the possibility of transforming and transcending human nature). He says, "Hope begins only when human beings start to realize that the kingdom of heaven, or whatever other name you care to give it, is within and can be experienced by anybody who's prepared to take the necessary trouble. That's the optimistic side of Christianity and the other world religions."

CHAPTER EIGHT

Dr. Obispo is suitably impressed when Jeremy reads that the fifth earl had three illegitimate children at the age of eighty-one. The notebook relates further sexual successes by reason of the earl's diet of carp gut, and also that the earl's housekeeper, Kate, is on the same carp diet. The fifth earl's scandalous conduct finally resulted in a warrant for his arrest; to escape prosecution the earl arranged his own funeral, with the body of an aged pauper taking his place in the coffin. He and Kate planned to live secretly in the subterranean retreat which he had outfitted for his experiments. Since the earl's retreat was in the house which formerly contained the Hauberk Papers, Dr. Obispo announces that he is going to England.

CHAPTER NINE

On his way back from the Beverly Pantheon, Jo Stoyte stops at the Children's Hospital, but even seeing the children does not make him happy. When he arrives at the castle and finds Virginia and Dr. Obispo in a compromising position near the swimming pool, he hesitates, undecided what to do. Unseen, he withdraws quietly and goes to look for his gun.

CHAPTER TEN

Pete considers all that Mr. Propter has said - the idea that "God is completely present only in the complete absence of what we call our humanity." Pete asks what he should do to find the real order of the world and liberty and peace. Then, returning to the castle, he goes immediately to the swimming pool.

Comment

Huxley brings the opposites together - Jo and Pete embodying, respectively, chaos and order, bondage and liberty, violence and peace.

Arriving at the swimming pool, Pete finds Virginia alone and crying, and tries to comfort her; thinking he is the doctor, Jo rushes in and shoots. Dr. Obispo arrives a few minutes later and finds Pete with a bullet through his head, Jo trying to staunch the blood with his handkerchief, and Virginia sobbing and praying. Mr. Stoyte pleads with the doctor to help him, and the doctor agrees to do so if the price is right.

AFTER MANY A SUMMER DIES THE SWAN

TEXTUAL ANALYSIS

PART THREE

CHAPTER ONE

Some time has passed since Pete's funeral. Mr. Propter and Jeremy are on their way to the dedication of the new Stoyte Auditorium at Tarzana College. They discuss Pete's sudden and premature death; neither had realized his heart was so bad. In his dedication speech Dr. Mulge makes reference to Mr. Stoyte - his generosity, his vision, his dedication to social service and culture - a source of inspiration to all.

CHAPTER TWO

Mr. Stoyte, Virginia, and Dr. Obispo are in London. Having made arrangements to hush up the circumstances of Pete's death,

Dr. Obispo is in command of the situation. The trip is made to satisfy the doctor's curiosity about the fifth earl and to get Jo and Virginia away from the castle and the memory of Pete's murder. On their way to see the two old Hauberk ladies, Dr. Obispo whistles and occasionally sings aloud; Virginia sits and sadly reminisces; and Mr. Stoyte dozes alone in the back seat.

Arriving at the estate, Dr. Obispo succeeds in entering the house, and leads Jo and Virginia down into cellarage. At the end of a short corridor is a door like the door of a death cell in a prison. Dr. Obispo looks in and then bursts into paroxysms of laughter. On the edge of a low bed sits the hunched-up figure of a man, his legs thickly covered with coarse hair, a filthy shirt his only garment. Another figure appears - a very old woman clothed in an old check garment and some glass beads. Dr. Obispo tells Jo and Virginia about the notebook, the carp gut, and the fact that the man is over two hundred years old. He sarcastically remarks that since the carp gut ensures longevity, Mr. Stoyte can start taking it at once. A few minutes later the fifth earl rises to his feet, stretches, scratches himself, and joins the female in the darkness. After much excited chattering and yelling and screaming, the two apes are quiet. Finally Mr. Stoyte speaks, "They look like they were having a good time. I mean in their own way, of course. Don't you think so, Obispo?" The doctor throws back his head and roars with laughter.

Comment

Jo Stoyte's willingness to revert to the level of the ape in order to achieve longevity expresses Huxley's conviction that man is beyond redemption. Man's desire to gratify self ultimately reaches a point where man is willing to discard completely those things which distinguish him from the animal.

AFTER MANY A SUMMER DIES THE SWAN

CHARACTER ANALYSES

CHIEF CHARACTERS

Jeremy Pordage

A middle-aged Englishman and a scholar, Jeremy is supposedly intelligent and well educated. But his superior mental ability does not help him or others to live fuller, more worthwhile lives. Huxley loathed the poses and inconsistencies of the modern intellectual, as can be seen in his development of the character of Jeremy. In many ways this caricature is the most devastating and sarcastic one presented in this novel.

Mr. Propter

As Huxley's spokesman in the novel, Mr. Propter's intelligence, wisdom, honesty, and charity contrast vividly with the stupidity, dishonesty, and immorality of the others. Like Jeremy, he is a scholar, but he uses his intelligence to better himself and to better mankind. In many ways Mr. Propter is Mr. Proper-Huxley believed that mankind should strive to emulate his virtues. A good part of the novel is devoted to presenting Mr. Propter's (and Huxley's) philosophy of life.

Jo Stoyte

Mr. Stoyte is a fabulously rich business tycoon who believes money can buy anything, and who hopes it might even buy immortality. He was a poor boy who made good - a self-made man. He gives to charity because it is tax-deductible; he collects art to compensate for his ignorance; he contributes to higher education to gain a reputation for philanthropy. Huxley presents Jo as the epitome of those who are vulgar, crude, and depraved - but wealthy. Ironically, society often applauds the type of individual Huxley is satirizing.

Virginia Maunciple

A perverse madonna, Virginia enjoys, meditates upon, and practices sex and saintliness, prayer and passion, in about equal proportions. She is scatter-brained, impulsive, fickle, sensuous. Huxley, does not condemn her for what she is or isn't - he sees her as a product of the place and the times. She is more to be pitied than blamed.

Dr. Sigmund Obispo

The first name is a clue - like Sigmund Freud, Dr. Obispo sees sex not as simply one aspect of life but as the most important and meaningful of man's activities. He considers romance, love, and marriage to be frivolous addenda. He is a medical doctor, but he is not interested in practicing medicine; he does research, not to benefit mankind but to benefit himself. Huxley pictures him as being similar to Jeremy - his intelligence is wasted because it is not used to benefit mankind or himself.

Peter Boone

Next to Mr. Propter, Peter is the most admirable and worthwhile character in the novel. He is idealistic and virtuous - but he is ineffective because of ignorance and lack of direction. Huxley represents him as the individual who is capable of living a worthwhile life if given guidance.

Mr. Herbert Mulge

The Principal (President) of Tarzana College is not interested in education, but in endowments. Having satirized the products of higher education (Jeremy and Dr. Obispo), Huxley now caricatures those concerned with directing higher education.

AFTER MANY A SUMMER DIES THE SWAN

ESSAY QUESTIONS AND ANSWERS

....

Question: Mr. Propter is the main character and Huxley's spokesman in *After Many a Summer*. What is the foundation of his "philosophy of life"?

Answer: In chapter eight, Mr. Propter meditates on "What is man?" The answer: "A nothingness surrounded by God; indigent and capable of God, filled with God if he so desires." For Mr. Propter the crux of the problem is "if he [man] so desires." This union with God is possible only if man is liberated from personality and liberated from time and craving. Mr. Propter seeks ways and means of achieving this liberation from self.

Question: Why is *After Many a Summer* sometimes considered an "extension" of *Eyeless in Gaza*?

Answer: Mr. Propter in *After Many a Summer* carries out many of the ideas which Anthony Beavis in *Eyeless in Gaza* was just becoming aware of. Anthony Beavis preaches a doctrine based on mysticism; Mr. Propter lives a life based on mysticism.

Anthony begins to realize that "Life and all being are one"; Mr. Propter goes one step further to seek "union with God." And, too, Mr. Propter goes a step further than Anthony when he not only talks about his beliefs, but also does something about them - he seeks ways of being self-sufficient and helps others to attain such freedom.

Question: Next to Mr. Propter, Jeremy Pordage is the most important character in the novel. Why does Huxley develop his character so completely?

Answer: Huxley uses Jeremy as a contrast to Mr. Propter - another instance of his "two-angled" view. Jeremy and Propter are comparable in age, education, social status, and intellectual achievement - yet how different they are! Propter is self-sufficient - Jeremy is mother-dominated; Mr. Propter participates actively in life - Jeremy shuns social contact (he prefers his books); Mr. Propter concerns himself with discovering the reality of existence - Jeremy is concerned with writing clever letters to his mother. Jeremy is a caricature of the modern intellectual whose education and intelligence has no effect on his own life or the life of others.

EYELESS IN GAZA

INTRODUCTION

Eyeless in Gaza is a morality story - a spiritual biography - the story of one man groping for a way of life that will bring meaning and purpose to his existence. Anthony Beavis is introduced as a sensuous, self-indulgent, detached philosopher. He views life cynically and has little respect or concern for anybody or anything. He loves no one because love demands sacrifice and commitment. But after he meets Dr. Miller, all this is changed. Anthony accepts his responsibility as a member of the human race and thereby finds peace and contentment. The title of the novel is taken from a line of Milton's bitter description of the fettered Samson: "Eyeless in Gaza at the mill with slaves." Like Samson, Anthony Beavis was bound by the Philistines the modern world's values and beliefs or lack of them.

In this novel Aldous Huxley switches back and forth in the time sequence, the **episodes** following the associations evoked in the memory of Anthony Beavis. In the novel Anthony comments on the associative process; he considers it analogous to a lunatic shuffling a pack of cards and dealing them out at random again and again. He reviews his conscious life and calls it a chaos - a pack of snapshots in the hands of a lunatic. Life has no purpose, no **rhyme** or reason - even as these remembrances of things past serve no purpose. But at times Anthony Beavis wonders if this picture gallery in his mind has some purpose - if there is a pattern and a meaning to these remembrances and to life.

In the first chapter Huxley presents Anthony in the process of looking through an assortment of photographs which recall certain events and certain people in his life. Huxley then moves backwards and forwards in time - a series of snapshots selected at random, yet each one related in some way to another. Thus the reader sees not only an isolated person or event which has influenced the main character, but also the influence this person or event continues to have. Anthony cannot escape his past - nor his future. In Four Quartets T.S. Eliot expressed this juxtaposition of time and reality thus: "Time present and time past are both perhaps present in time future, and time future contained in time past."

In *Eyeless in Gaza* Aldous Huxley is concerned with cause and effect - and with the unity of all life. In the words of Anthony Beavis, "Each organism is unique. Unique and yet united with all other organisms in the sameness of its ultimate parts: Unique above a substratum of physical identity." The handling of time in this novel and the consequent juxtaposition of events and characters makes the reader aware of cause and effect at work even though the main character is not aware of it until the last chapter. Finally Anthony realizes that since he has found peace with himself and with the world, he has achieved unity - unity with other lives and unity with all being.

The year is 1934. The novel opens with Anthony Beavis rummaging through snapshots he has accumulated over the years - photographs of himself as a child, photographs of friends and relatives, photographs recording certain events in his life. He speaks of them as old corpses - reminders of his earlier life and some of the people and events who influenced him. Anthony sees himself in various poses, in various situations, with various people. Anthony Beavis - who is forty-two when the novel opens and forty-four when it closes - is a composite of these mental pictures, the result of many influences.

In the first chapter Anthony reminisces about his life and considers the kind of person he is: "Suppressing his curiosity, he went on stubbornly playing the part he had long since assigned himself - the part of the detached philosopher, of the preoccupied man of science who doesn't see the things that to everyone else are obvious." Anthony Beavis, the detached philosopher and preoccupied man of science, examines life so closely he is unable to see its reality. He can manipulate ideas, but he lacks self-knowledge and the desire to accomplish anything.

EYELESS IN GAZA

TEXTUAL ANALYSIS

OLDER, BUT NOT WISER (1933)

Helen, Mary Amberley's daughter, becomes Anthony's mistress (like mother, like daughter). At first she thinks it is love, but later she realizes that Anthony does not want to love or be loved. Their arrangement involves no fuss - just a simple arrangement based on the needs of each, but with each one unconcerned about the needs of the other. However, an extraordinary occurrence climaxes their affair - while they are lying naked on the roof, a plane passes overhead and a dog plummets to earth and smashes near them. The blood and gore sickens Helen, brings to mind her horror of the animal and physical elements of life, and results in her leaving Anthony. He does not understand that she is leaving him because she sees herself as an animal.

A few days later Mark Staithes comes to see Anthony; Helen had told him what happened. Anthony has been examining his life and his values since the **episode** of the dog - he sees himself as a weak and timid person. Mark tells him he should commit himself to something - he should risk something. Anthony finally agrees to accompany Mark to Mexico to participate in an attempt at bringing about a revolution in a Central American country.

They arrive in Panama; Mark considers their first misadventures quite humorous, but Anthony is depressed and humiliated. He had hoped to be shaken out of his negative view of life, but their experiences do not provide the necessary stimulus. The day for the uprising is set, and they begin their trek over the mountains to rendezvous with Don Jorge, the leader of the rebels. On the second day Mark's leg is seriously injured when his mule stumbles and falls; infection sets in and Anthony goes for a doctor. By chance he meets James Miller, a medical doctor and anthropologist who has been traveling through the area. Miller amputates the leg and saves Mark's life, but instead of being grateful Mark berates himself and everybody else for his failure to arrive in time for the uprising.

Anthony is impressed by James Miller - anthropologist, doctor, philosopher, humanitarian, pacifist - and by his beliefs. Dr. Miller eats like a Buddhist and thinks like a Buddhist, and has found the peace and contentment that has eluded Anthony. The doctor believes that if men are treated as men, they will behave as men; if you treat them well, they will treat you well. Mark ridicules this idealism, but Anthony says he wants to join Miller in his crusade to change the world by changing the individuals that make up the world.

EYELESS IN GAZA

TEXTUAL ANALYSIS

TRYING TO FIND HIMSELF (1934)

The three return to London, and Anthony embarks on a new life. He becomes an active and positive pacifist and supports Miller's crusade by contributing time and money. Anthony writes pamphlets which express their beliefs and concerns and also speaks out publicly for their cause. He becomes an ardent disciple of Buddha, desiring to improve himself and the world. At times he is tempted to return to his old habits of thinking, living, and feeling that the world is a senseless place where nothing can be done, but he remains true to his new philosophy of life. At Dr. Miller's suggestion Anthony keeps a journal, and records his activities, impressions, and reactions.

Anthony's journal traces his spiritual growth - in Dr. Miller's words, "Self-knowledge, an essential preliminary to self-change." Believing that mind and body are one, Anthony practices physical control as a prelude to control of impulse and feeling. Anthony wants to be free - to be "calm and at peace, innocent of all craving, all ambition." Dr. Miller tells him this is possible through awareness and control - to learn proper use one must first inhibit all improper uses of the self. By developing the power to inhibit and control, he believes it becomes easier to inhibit undesirable impulses and easier to put good intentions into practice. Anthony for the first time in his life experiences peace and contentment.

Dr. Miller believes that pacifist propaganda must be aimed at people and their governments. He believes that all men are capable of love for other human beings; that limitations we place on this love - personal dislike, class feeling, national hatred, color prejudice - can be overcome; that love expressing itself in good treatment breeds love. Since a nation is composed of individuals, nations will change their policies only if individuals change their beliefs. Both Anthony and Dr. Miller preach these principles at public rallies. The majority of people attracted to these gatherings are merely curious; a few are sincerely interested in the doctrine of pacifism; and a few others come to heckle and abuse the speakers.

Anthony finds great satisfaction in what he is doing - he has escaped the negativism he formerly felt, and life for him seems more complete and more rewarding. He sees the purpose of existence as the unity of mankind, the uniting of all life. Suddenly he realizes "there was nothing he could do but would affect them all, enemies and friends alike - for good, if what he did were good, for evil if it were wrong."

At last he accepts life, believing that regardless of what happens to him, all will be well.

EYELESS IN GAZA

TEXTUAL ANALYSIS

CHILDHOOD (1902 - 1903)

....

When Anthony is eleven years old his mother dies, and he attends her funeral with his father and his Uncle James. Anthony feels lost among these grownups, these giants and is bewildered by his father's attempt to make him more aware of the tragedy of his mother's untimely death. (John Beavis is concerned that the proper amount of sorrow and respect for the dead be shown.)

Anthony is glad to return to St. Dominic's, the boarding school he has been attending.

The boys are all very decent to him on his return; baby-faced "Benger Beavis" is now a source of curiosity and wonder since his mother has died. Only Brian Foxe, old "Horse-Face," is able to express his sympathy. Anthony likes and admires Brian because he is a "good fellow" and has the courage of his convictions, but he still joins the others in ridiculing Brian for these same attributes.

Anthony begins to spend most of his holidays with Brian and Mrs. Foxe. Her marriage had been unhappy, and since her husband's death she has lavished all her love and affection on Brian and all unfortunates with whom she comes in contact; Anthony unwillingly shares in this beneficence. Anthony enjoys these visits: away from school he can treat Brian as a friend; at school he feels compelled to join the others in ridiculing Brian's stammer and Brian's virtue.

John Beavis tries to keep alive the sorrow and pain he felt at the death of his wife, but to no avail. Before a year has passed, his memories of her are fading, his sorrow and grief are assuaged, and his interests are centered around Pauline Gannett, a plump and pretty young woman of twenty-seven. Meanwhile, Brian and Anthony are preparing for their scholarship examinations at Eton.

EYELESS IN GAZA

TEXTUAL ANALYSIS

APPROACHING MIDDLE AGE (1926 - 1928)

After Brian's death, Anthony quarrels with Mary Amberley and they avoid each other. After twelve years an invitation to dinner changes all that - Anthony accepts, anxious to see how she has changed. Mary is now forty-three, and her two girls, Joyce and Helen, are twenty-two and eighteen, respectively. The dinner party brings together some interesting characters and leads to some interesting combinations: Gerry Watchett is introduced as Mary's latest lover (later he swindles her); Mark Staithes (one of Anthony's classmates) is a Bolshevist; Hugh Ledwidge (another classmate) later marries Helen. Anthony is amused and bemused by the various situations and circumstances and again becomes involved with the Amberleys.

EYELESS IN GAZA

TEXTUAL ANALYSIS

THE YOUNG GENTLEMAN (1912 - 1914)

Anthony and Brian's friendship remains firm in spite of the Widening gap in their beliefs, ideas, and behavior. Anthony wants to be free, to be uncommitted, to be self-sufficient, with obligations to no person, thing, or idea. Brian has wholeheartedly embraced Christianity, and his very existence is a living expression of its ideals. Anthony wants to live on an intellectual plane and avoid any emotional involvement; Brian wants to live a spiritual life on earth and avoid any immoral sexual involvement.

At this time both are experiencing the joys and sorrows of a first love: Anthony is having an affair with Mary Amberley, an experienced "older woman' who is a divorcee and the mother of two young girls, Joyce and Helen; Brian has found his ideal in Joan Thurslay, a minister's daughter: Anthony is pleased by the physical pleasure that his relationship with Mary offers. Brian, on the other hand, is distressed by the sexual impulses he feels towards Joan - they intrude upon and ruin the spiritual ideal of love.

This affair with Anthony is not Mary's first such escapade; she finds him attractive and amusing and enjoys the power she wields over him. Anthony is grateful for Mary's attention and for the satisfaction she gives him, and he is anxious to please her. Her playfulness and his desire to please a little later indirectly bring about Brian's suicide.

Mrs. Foxe has molded Brian to her image and likeness - she presents herself as the epitome of virtue and Christian charity, and Brian admires her and wants to emulate the ideals she seems to personify. He does not realize that her charity and virtue are but disguises for her selfishness - her desire to keep Brian for herself. She arranges to keep Brian from marrying Joan and creates great unhappiness for both of them - they begin to feel their love, their desires, their whole relationship is somehow wrong, is in some way vile. Both Brian and Joan turn to Anthony for advice.

Mary is greatly amused when Anthony tells her about Brian and Joan. Brian feels that any pleasurable physical contact - even kissing - is wrong; Joan feels that this is a physical manifestation of love and is not wrong. Mary tells Anthony that he should seduce Joan to prove her womanhood and his manhood. (After two years, Mary finds Anthony rather dull and feels that this little intrigue could be amusing.) Anthony protests, but she insists; if he doesn't do it, she will never speak to him again.

In this venture, Anthony is successful, too successful, for Joan thinks he is in love with her and she, with him. She says she will write to Brian, explain what has happened, and break the engagement. Anthony does not have the nerve to tell her his real feelings and says he will go to Langdale and tell Brian - he hopes to be able to explain that the whole thing was a "lark," but he realizes that this will be difficult, if not impossible, to do.

Anthony is distressed when he sees Brian; his working and studying coupled with his attempt to achieve perfection have resulted in great physical and mental deterioration. Brian continues to "push" himself, feeling sure that the spiritual can master the physical. Anthony stays with him for several days but cannot bring himself to tell Brian what happened between him and Joan.

On the fourth day Anthony goes off by himself; when he returns he finds that Brian has gone for a walk. When Brian doesn't return, Anthony begins to be concerned, looks around the cottage, and finds the letter Brian has left for him. Brian has enclosed the letter he had received from Joan that morning which told of her feeling for Anthony; the next morning they find Brian's body at the foot of a cliff.

EYELESS IN GAZA

CHARACTER ANALYSES

Anthony Beavis

As noted in the introduction, Huxley presents Anthony as a modern man who has found a purpose and meaning to existence. We are made aware of the forces that have molded him and of the people who have influenced him. Anthony expresses Huxley's belief that man can better himself only by individual effort and the assumption of individual responsibility.

Dr. James Miller

Anthropologist, humanitarian, pacifist, medical doctor - Dr. Miller is presented as an idealist and an ideal. By his teaching and by his example, he helps Anthony to find himself.

John Beavis

Anthony's father is presented as an ineffective intellectual whose ideas and ideals come to naught. He represents the man of learning who is of benefit to no one, not even himself. (Each of these characters represents an attitude or idea which Huxley condemns as unworthy of man.)

Brian Foxe

A classmate and friend of Anthony's, he is the idealist unable to live his ideal. Brian tries to completely subdue the body and live by the spirit, thereby negating part of man's nature.

Mrs. Foxe

Brian's mother uses love as a means of control - she has perverted man's noblest impulse. Her apparently virtuous actions disguise her treachery and selfishness.

Mary Amberley

Anthony's first mistress is a study in moral disintegration. Her whole existence centers around her attempt to gratify the senses and her sexual impulses.

Mark Staithes

A revolutionist by temperament and a Bolshevist by choice, Mark escapes negativism through action. For him action is the most important thing - doing, not thinking.

EYELESS IN GAZA

CRITICAL COMMENTARY

Aldous Huxley will never be called a "great novelist," but he certainly deserves to be called an "important novelist." Beginning with the publication of *Crome Yellow* in 1921 and continuing through the twenty-seventh printing of the Bantam Classic edition of *Brave New World* in 1963, the continuing interest in his work seems to leave little doubt of Huxley's importance as a novelist. How important and influential a novelist he is depends on the criteria used for evaluation purposes. A brief look at some of the comments about his novels may aid us in making our own evaluation of his importance.

With the publication of *Antic Hay* in 1923, Huxley's reputation as a novelist was established. The critics and the public were impressed by his vivid characterizations, by his cynical mockery of religion, conventional morality, and romantic love (his writing reflected the disillusionment of the time), and, most of all, by his success in making the novel "alive." Critics still consider *Antic Hay* his best novel - somehow Huxley was never again able to create characters that were more than mere mouthpieces for his ideas.

The following quotation from the July 1935 issue of the *Sewanee Review* (from "Aldous Huxley's Humanism" by Winfield H. Rogers) indicates the direction Huxley's writings were taking: "Mr. Huxley stands out as one of the most important social thinkers, as well as critics and creative writers, of our time." Note the order of importance - social thinker, critic, creative writer. Because Huxley himself considered his role as social commentator most important, he was primarily interested in using the novel as another medium for the dissemination of his ideas. Perhaps because his novel *Antic Hay* seemed to portend greater things to come, the critics never forgave him for his lack of concern with the novel as a novel and his overconcern with using the novel as his soapbox.

Huxley's shortcomings as a novelist have been noted by many critics. The following comment by David Daiches in *The Novel and the Modern World* (1939) is typical: "Huxley is not a novelist; he has never mastered - is not really interested in - even the elements of form and structure in fiction. His novels are either a series of character sketches or simple fables or tracts." This comment is certainly true, but it would be a mistake to think that Huxley was unaware of these "shortcomings."

In chapter 22 of *Point Counter Point*, Philip Quarles, Huxley's alter ego, discusses the "novel of ideas." Much of what he says expresses Huxley's concerns when writing a novel and the subsequent shortcomings noted by critics: "The character of each personage must be implied, as far as possible, in the ideas of which he is the mouthpiece.... You must write about people who have ideas to express - which excludes all but about .01 per cent of the human race.... The great defect of the novel of ideas is that it is a made-up affair." If we are willing to accept Huxley on his own terms, we can profit much from what he has to say, and we should be duly impressed by what he has done.

The most widely read and in some ways the most important of Huxley's novels is *Brave New World*. As an example of science fiction, it is outstanding; as social **satire**, it is devastating; as a perennial "best seller," it is phenomenal. If only because it has been widely read, the influence that this novel has had cannot be measured; to dismiss this novel as a "minor work by a minor author" would be absurd.

Eyeless in Gaza failed to attract the attention and to wield the influence which it in many ways deserves. Few novelists are willing or able to discuss the eternal questions which are astir in their age and community. Huxley is at least willing to try. In the July 19, 1936, *New York Times* review of *Eyeless in Gaza*, J. Donald Adams wrote: "... he has written a novel which is at least the equal, if not the superior, in intellectual and spiritual content, of any in our time ... the picture of an individual man groping for a way of life that will bring meaning and purpose to his existence." Huxley comes to grips with an important question - he attempts to give a satisfactory answer. Whether we agree with him or not is unimportant - we should be thankful that he has at least attempted to find and express a satisfactory answer.

The other two novels discussed in this study guide - *Point Counter Point* and *After Many a Summer* - have certain virtues. As novels they are entertaining and, in some ways, enlightening. Huxley's comments are often humorous, his range of interests is impressive, and his manifestations of the incongruous quality of life are thought-provoking. *Point Counter Point* is also a quite remarkable, albeit at times tedious, achievement as a literary work (a device similar to that used by Andre Gide in *The Counterfeiters*). As a "way-out" story of the ultimate in pleasure-seeking, *After Many A Summer* often hits home.

Huxley writes with a pen in one hand and a scalpel in the other - there is no weakness of human nature he does not expose. But as John Atkins noted in his book, *Aldous Huxley: A Literary Study* (1956), "No other contemporary author is so critical of the society in which he lives, and yet he frequently expresses a conviction that this society, however rotten, has the power to improve itself." As Anthony Beavis learned in *Eyeless in Gaza*, "Self-knowledge is an essential preliminary to self-change." Huxley's novels might well help us to know ourselves better - and to change.

EYELESS IN GAZA

ESSAY QUESTIONS AND ANSWERS

....

Question: Why is this novel called a spiritual biography?

Answer: *Eyeless in Gaza* recounts Anthony Beavis' transformation from a sensuous, self-indulgent, detached philosopher to a responsible member of the human race. We see the people and events that influenced him, his struggle to find a purpose and meaning to life, his hesitations and doubts once he had made his decision. Finally we see him content and at peace with himself. In many ways this novel recounts Huxley's own search for a purpose and meaning to life.

Question: Why does Huxley move backwards and forwards in time?

Answer: The shift in time emphasizes the "unity of life" which Anthony comes to understand and appreciate at the end of the novel. Huxley juxtaposes time to show how various characters and events were united - how Anthony was influenced physically, mentally, and spiritually be seemingly irrelevant happenings. As Anthony notes in chapter three, "The thirty-five years of his conscious life made themselves immediately known to him as a chaos - a pack of snapshots in the hands of a lunatic." Until Anthony realizes that "unity was the beginning and unity the end," his life is a chaos. The novel is structured to illustrate at one and the same time unity and chaos.

BIBLIOGRAPHY

General Background And Criticism

"Aldous Huxley," in *Writers at Work; The Paris Review Interviews: Second Series.* New York (1963), 193 - 214. (Contains some interesting off-the-cuff remarks.)

Atkins, John. *Aldous Huxley: A Literary Study.* London, 1956. (One of the best studies available.)

Brooke, Jocelyn. *Aldous Huxley.* London, 1954. (A pamphlet containing much valuable information.)

Buck, Philo. "Sight to the Blind - Aldous Huxley," in *Directions in Contemporary Literature.* New York (1942), 169 - 191.

Bullough, Geoffrey. "Aspects of Aldous Huxley," *English Studies*, XXX (October 1949), 233 - 243.

Burgum, Edwin. "Aldous Huxley and His Dying Swan," in *The Novel and the World's Dilemma.* New York (1947), 140 - 156.

Daiches, David. "Aldous Huxley," in *The Novel and the Modern World.* Chicago (1939), 188 - 210. (Some perceptive commentary; often quoted.)

Edgar, Pelham. "Aldous Huxley," in *The Art of the Novel from 1700 to the Present Time*. New York (1933), 278 - 293. (Attempts to put Huxley in perspective.)

Estrich, H. W. "Jesting Pilate Tells the Answer," *Sewanee Review*, XLVII (January 1939), 63 - 81. (Discusses Huxley's role as social commentator.)

Frierson, William. *The English Novel in Transition 1885 - 1940*. Norman, Okla., 1942 (see index). (Shows Huxley in perspective.)

Glicksberg, Charles. "Aldous Huxley: Art and Mysticism," *Prairie Schooner*, XXVII (Winter, 1953), 344 - 353.

Godfrey, F. R. "The Essence of Aldous Huxley," *English Studies*, XXXII (June, 1951), 97 - 106.

Hall, James. *The Tragic Comedians*. Bloomington, Ind., 1963 (see index). (Some important comments.)

Hamilton, Robert. "The Challenge of Aldous Huxley," *Horizon*, XVII (June, 1948), 441 - 456. (Discusses Huxley's attempt to find answers.)

Henderson, Alexander. *Aldous Huxley*. London, 1935. (Many perceptive comments on Huxley's earlier work.)

Hoffman, F. J. "Aldous Huxley and the Novel of Ideas," *College English*, VIII (December 1946), 129 - 137. (Further **exposition** of Huxley as commentator-novelist.)

Hopper, Stanley R. *Spiritual Problems in Contemporary Literature*. New York, 1957 (see index). (Discusses Huxley's quest for answers.)

Koorstra, J. "Aldous Huxley," *English Studies*, XVIII (October 1931), 161 - 175.

Lawrence, D. H. *The Letters of D. H. Lawrence*. New York, 1932 (see index). (Many letters offer valuable comments on Huxley as author and friend.)

Maurois, Andre. "Aldous Huxley," in *Prophets and Poets*. New York (1935), 285 - 312.

Muir, Edwin. "Aldous Huxley," in *Transition: Essays on Contemporary Literature*. New York (1926), 101 - 113. (Many perceptive comments applicable to Huxley's later development.)

Nagarajam, S. "Religion in Three Recent Novels of Aldous Huxley," *Modern Fiction Studies*, V (Spring, 1959), 153 - 165. (Concern with the influence of mysticism on Huxley's writings.)

O'Faolain, Sean. "Huxley and Waugh" in *The Vanishing Hero*, Boston (1956), 3 - 44.

Quennell, Peter. "D. H. Lawrence and Aldous Huxley," in *The English Novelists*. London (1936), 245 - 258. (Discusses Lawrence's influence on Huxley.)

Savage, Derek S. "Aldous Huxley and the Dissociation of Personality," *Sewanee Review*, LV (Autumn, 1947), 537 - 568. (Discusses Huxley's withdrawal from society.)

Tindall, William Y. "The Trouble with Aldous Huxley," *American Scholar*, XI (Autumn, 1942), 452 - 464.

Tindall, William Y. "Hunt for a Father," in *Forces in Modern British Literature*, 1885 - 1946. New York (1947), 185 - 223. (Whatever Tindall says is usually worthwhile.)

Other Works By Huxley

As noted earlier, Huxley was a more gifted essayist than he was a novelist. Consequently his novels often simply touch upon a particular idea; it was in his essays that he most fully and logically developed his philosophy and beliefs. The collections of essays and individual essays listed below will help the student to gain a better understanding and appreciation of many of the ideas alluded to in the four novels discussed in this study guide.

Brave New World Revisited. New York, 1958.

Ends and Means, an Enquiry into the Nature of Ideals and into the Methods Employed for Their Realization. New York, 1937.

"Fashions in Love," in *Do What You Will.* London, 1929.

The Perennial Philosophy. London, 1946.

"The Traveller's-Eye View," in *Forum*, LXXIV (November 1925) 697 - 703.

"Vulgarity in Literature," in *Music at Night, and Other Essays.* New York, 1931.

www.ingramcontent.com/pod-product-compliance
Lightning Source LLC
LaVergne TN
LVHW021715060526
838200LV00050B/2683